AF386250

FOR EVERYONE WHO LET ME IN.

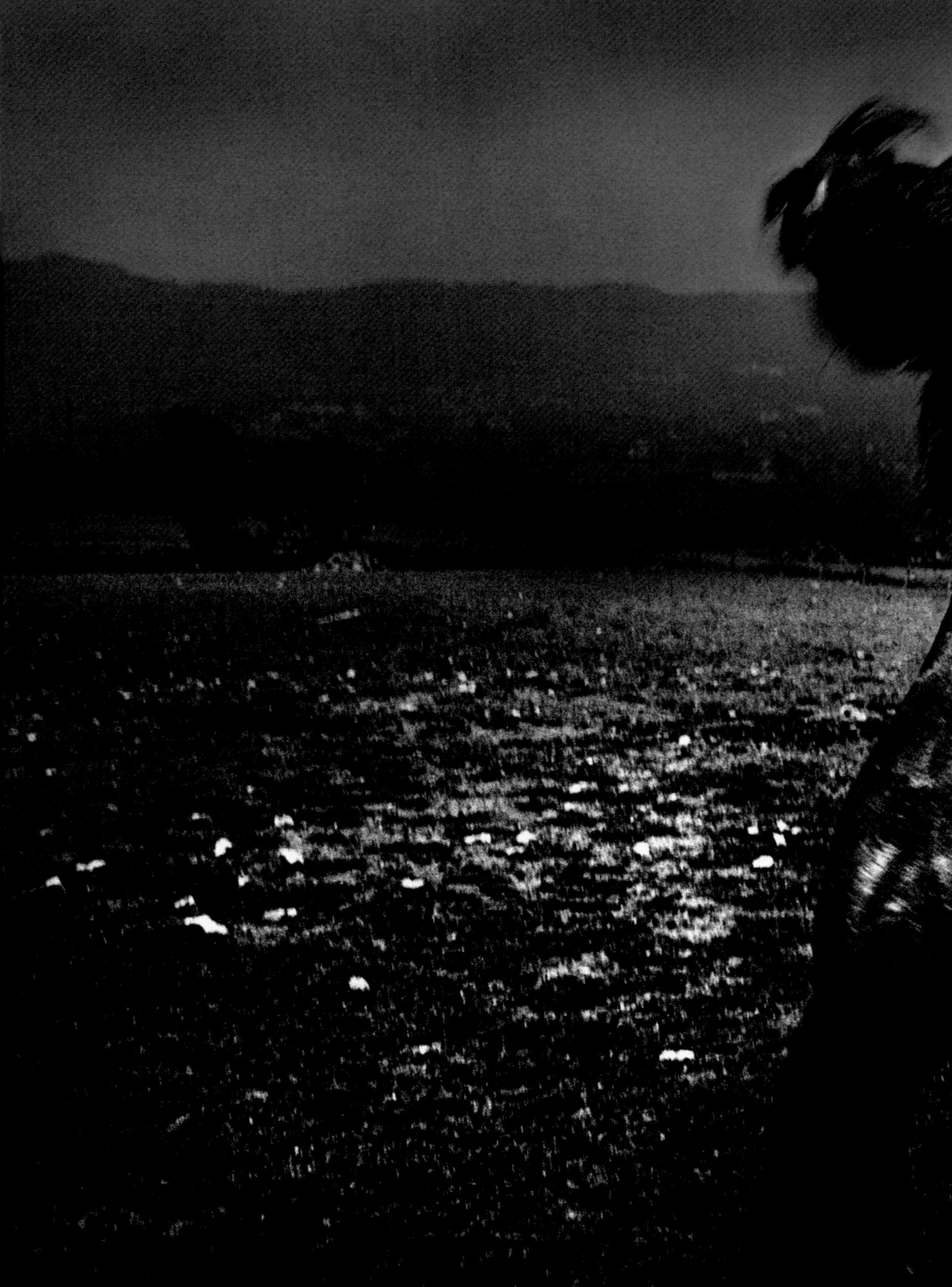

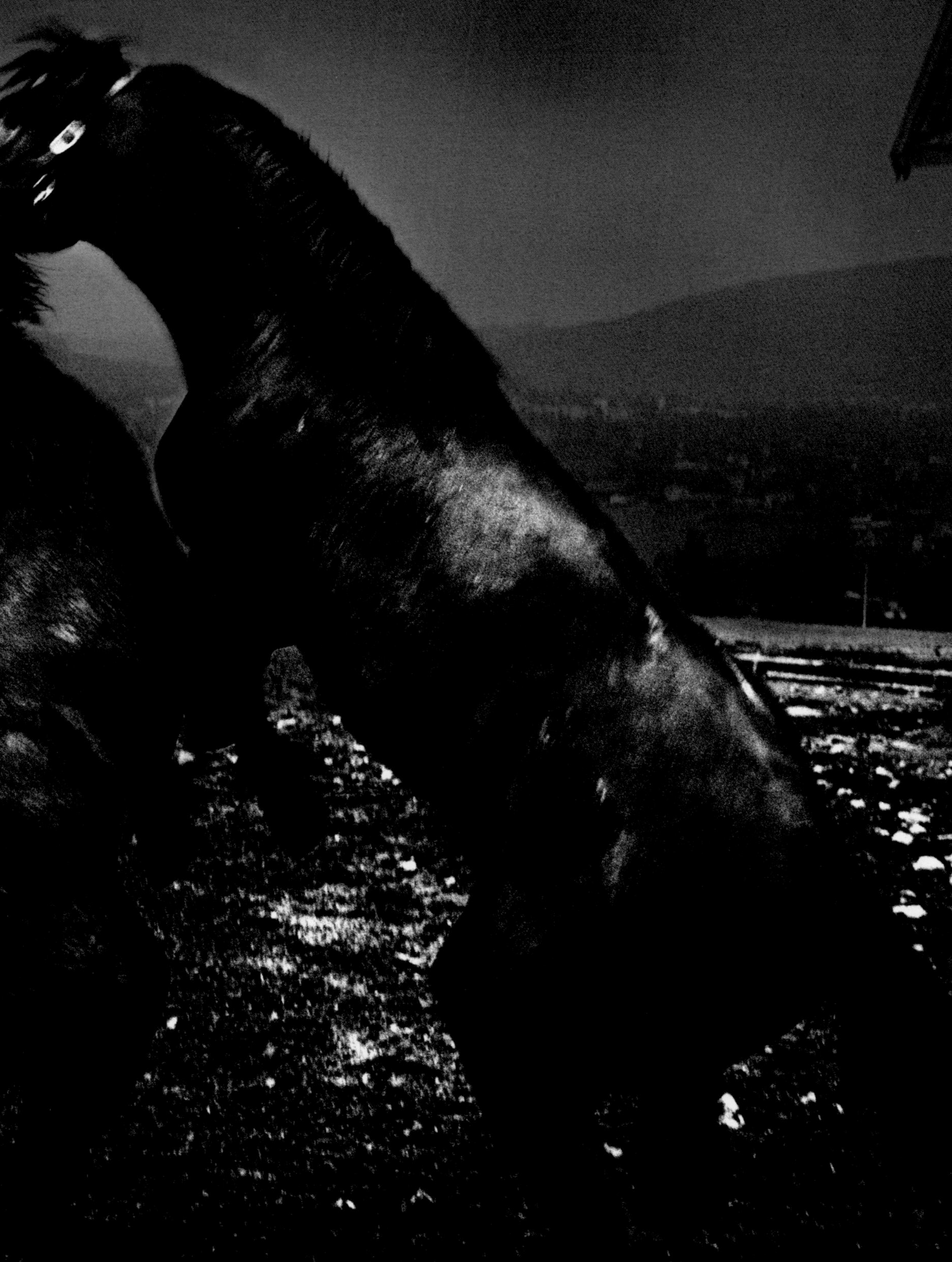

SURROUNDED BY *NO ONE*

MARGARET M. DE LANGE

TROLLEY

THE HORSEPOWER OF DESIRE

ARNO RAFAEL MINKKINEN

It happens every now and then around midnight on long haul drives back home to New England that I get the urge to latch on to a passing speedster—BMW, Mercedes, and the Jag sorts—my speedometer quickly surging to pick up their pace. Sometimes we'll race neck and neck, or one of us drops back as the other presses forward. Passing what remains of the slowpoke packs still on the road is a given. But most often it's just the two of us, one centered in the other's rear-view mirror and vice versa. There's no power play. We are 80 mile-per-hour equals.

The unspoken agreement is to live outside the law, take our chances with danger, joined at the fender hips like chariots out of *Ben Hur.* Inevitably one or the other's GPS forces the sudden parting: a flick of a turn signal to say goodbye.

Most people we see we see but once, just a glimpse of a face, perhaps on the metro, or on a bus, or coming out of a doctor's office, through the mirror of a fast food checkout line grabbing a sack of hamburgers. Depending on how much we travel, the totality of faces staring back at us at any moment is impossible to know. But on the night road, something does stick; a semblance of recognition is made. Maybe it is because we are both faceless. We concur in our unspoken embrace of anonymity and lawlessness through the lure of horsepower. Surely I would never go on such blind date cruises with slow cars.

Lying on a couch in the middle of the night, a thirtyish woman wiggles her way out of skirt and panties to reveal the fullness of a waiting, quivering derriere. Surrounded by no one. Two women embrace in a kiss no one is present to see. Two men do the same, one clutching a vigilant canine sentinel to confirm the fact. *Get the hell out,* the dog barks. Four photographs later, we hear off camera the echo of a hard slamming door. What we are shown is a burst of tears, the face of a woman. *Fuck you,* she just finished shouting. And now, only the misery of her loneliness stands naked before our eyes. We can imagine hearing what her partner spat back moments before the door got hammered: *Up yours!* In the photograph, the woman retreats to the hollow, empty nothingness of selfhood where we all eventually hold court in the midst of our own personal tragedies, surrounded by no one. A faceless couple sits at the edge of a bed. The off-camera man's giant fork of a hand rests not on her knee, where it ought to be, but on his own fucking thigh. Are we better off loving ourselves than taking care of someone else's throbbing libido? The androgynous figure in the photograph next door isn't doing a terrific job either—masturbating like a neophyte somewhere in the crack of the night. Scars and stitches, birthmarks and punches, noses that bleed like leaking faucets, faces that cars could have driven across stare out from a world no one has license to see. Because we are all, in fact, surrounded by no one. That face, our face, is ours alone.

So imagine it's just you aboard a crowded bus sitting next to a window and heading for the last stop of the bus route when suddenly a stranger takes the seat beside you. After some time, the bus begins emptying out; more people are getting off than are getting on and pretty soon there are just two people on the bus: you and your stranger. At what point then—the obvious question—do you strike up a conversation? Or do you just pretend to be asleep? Do we ever really step outside of ourselves?

Who are the people who inhabit the underworlds of these pages, the midnight tunnels with only one lightbulb to see by? There is anguish, despondency, rarely a glimpse of joy or a glimmer of hope and never a reason why, just the emotional and physical beatings and abuse these bodies and souls seem to have endured.

How did life begin for them? I often imagine such questions when looking at a photograph of an adult and peel away the life lived to imagine the child underneath, the person he or she once was. Or I turn it around. Saints or sinners, it's impossible to tell. I had a friend in Brooklyn when I was twelve with whom I played roller-skate hockey in the schoolyard. Bloodied to the bone, the guy competed to win no matter what, sniffed glue, and eventually wound up on the front page of the *Daily News* with a bold, screaming, one-word headline: EXECUTED.

When visiting relatives in the far reaches of Finland, I love pouring through the stacks of family albums they often pile up on my lap. You know the kind I mean: the faded black, double-weight pages with white-framed images—deckle-edged and dog-eared— clinging to photo corners hanging on like loose old teeth. My hosts love to point out the people they still know, but I am much more curious about the person hiding behind the lens, the person who is not in the picture.

Much in the same way, the author behind the lens of this family album of sorts raises my curiosity with every page my eyes suck in. Margaret M. de Lange's presence in the book becomes all the more visible by her very absence. I imagine for a moment what would happen if God had a camera. What kind of photographs would we get? I suppose Sunday school yearbook stuff, but Margaret M. de Lange has chosen to seek out the dark side of the moon. That much we know about her.

Through our email correspondence, de Lange offers no information about the subjects of her photographs any more than she does about herself. I am reluctant to inquire sensing perhaps that her caption-less photographs are intended to be just that, faces without names or histories, to be seen by us, and us alone.

As a college freshman, I chose to keep a single dormitory room so I could study uninterrupted but also so I could be alone—*surrounded by no one*—with the great erotic literature an English major would have at their disposal to consume in blissful isolation. It wasn't Playboys or Penthouses that I took to bed to stir my juvenile penile desires, but Henry Miller and James Joyce. There, under the covers, I was under Molly Bloom's petticoats and in her bloomers, especially during the *Ulysses* closer, that breathless, 45-page, single-sentence soliloquy, the greatest erotic email of the 20th century. Molly never failed to raise my erections. In the juiciest parts, I was alone with a woman who had no face yet was more real than most people walking and breathing ever are, my Molly, whose skirts got hiked as high as I wanted, her dripping underpants visible to me and me alone. I could reread such passages anytime I wanted and see her underwear over and over again. In de Lange's photographs, the narrative pull of the images provide the same tingling sensations of being alive, for better or for worse as the individual pictures dictate. In a world that was so artificial and fake back then as it is today, I found oneness with the self through the erotic escapades of my beloved author's characters. I was J.D. Salinger's Holden Caulfield in love with Joyce's Molly Bloom and likely, deep down inside, still am.

Tracing the sources of inspiration from one photographer to another provides rich and fascinating anchor points to understanding new work. It is a bit like the memory card game we played as kids. Where have I seen that image before? August Sander, Lisette Model, and Diane Arbus are the classic examples of inspiration and pushed boundaries working powerfully in tandem. In this sense, Margaret M. de Lange prowls the same mean streets, sad cafés, and half-star hotels as Anders Petersen and his teacher, Christer Strömholm. But what in this apparently man's world (think Robert Frank and Eugene Richards in America) does Margaret M. de Lange bring to the table? What boundaries does she push and shove aside? If Petersen solicits the encounter, thereby making the image happen, de Lange arrives to witness the aftermath. I see her plopping her camera bag down like a suitcase and staying a while. It makes a big difference for me, because with her photographs I often—but not always—get a model release with the image, a permission note allowing me to look as long as I want. This is not to say that the power of such photographs is any stronger for this trait, it's just a matter of sensing a welcome mat and being invited inside that I appreciate.

Aftermath becomes the modus operandi here. Like a forensic sleuth checking the hour with a finger in the coffee cup, timing is the key. The famous crime scene hunter Weegee of New York got there so fast his camera was folded away by the time the police arrived. But there is no hurry here to cover any bodies; the opposite, in fact, is more likely. Nonetheless, de Lange frames her images with quick reflexes and spontaneity adding cinematic tension and credible immediacy. But the camera doesn't cut away either. It lingers like an Ingmar Bergman film does, never letting us off the hook, even after something explosive, or tender for that matter, has happened. Suddenly we are looking down from a ceiling where on a rumpled bed sheet the elongated torso of a still very beautiful woman acknowledges and encourages a staring contest. With a Modigliani twist of the hip she flips her sex away, yet the half-stockings still wrapped about her ankles as much as the twisted bed sheets belie what likely happened moments earlier. How Margaret M. de Lange manages to arrive in people's homes and lives at such moments is like asking the magician to explain how the saw made such a clean, bloodless slice through the torso. The photographs remain unanswered riddles. How can an arrow pierce a heart and a belly button at the same time?

The frenzied graininess of much of Margaret M. de Lange's work—a product of emulsion speed unable to keep up with life speed—also lends her imagery its filmic urgency. Tough-guy grittiness aside, de Lange's use of the hard sandpaper look is often tempered by the interruption of emotionally charged soft landing spots seen with razor sharp clarity. The word *Pappa 26.01.50,* below the back of a woman's neck, or the deer-in-the-headlights eyes of a bewildered man as if apprehended for some nameless crime he will never know he committed, repeat themselves over and over again in these tightrope walker images of desire and consequence.

Is this what we look like when all panic lets loose, when anger escalates to a thrown hammer, when humiliation becomes an open wound, when lust demands the do-or-die victory we know it will get?

And so I am left with this book on my lap. Yes, it is indeed a family album. No, I don't know who any of these people are—anymore than I would know my nightriders—but I remain deeply curious to know more about the feverishly talented documentarian I have come to trust.

Dead bodies don't come back to life but dead people in old photographs do. The children in Margaret M. de Lange's photographs, fifty or a hundred years from now, will surely be looking back to a time of strange joys and inerasable sorrows. We like to think the world is becoming a better place. Perhaps it will become that. Let's hope. But for now, *Surrounded by no one* is a brave and beautiful benchmark to have in hand as a moral compass, a book of hard-lived lives seen through the vision of a photographer who appears to embrace everything and judges nothing.

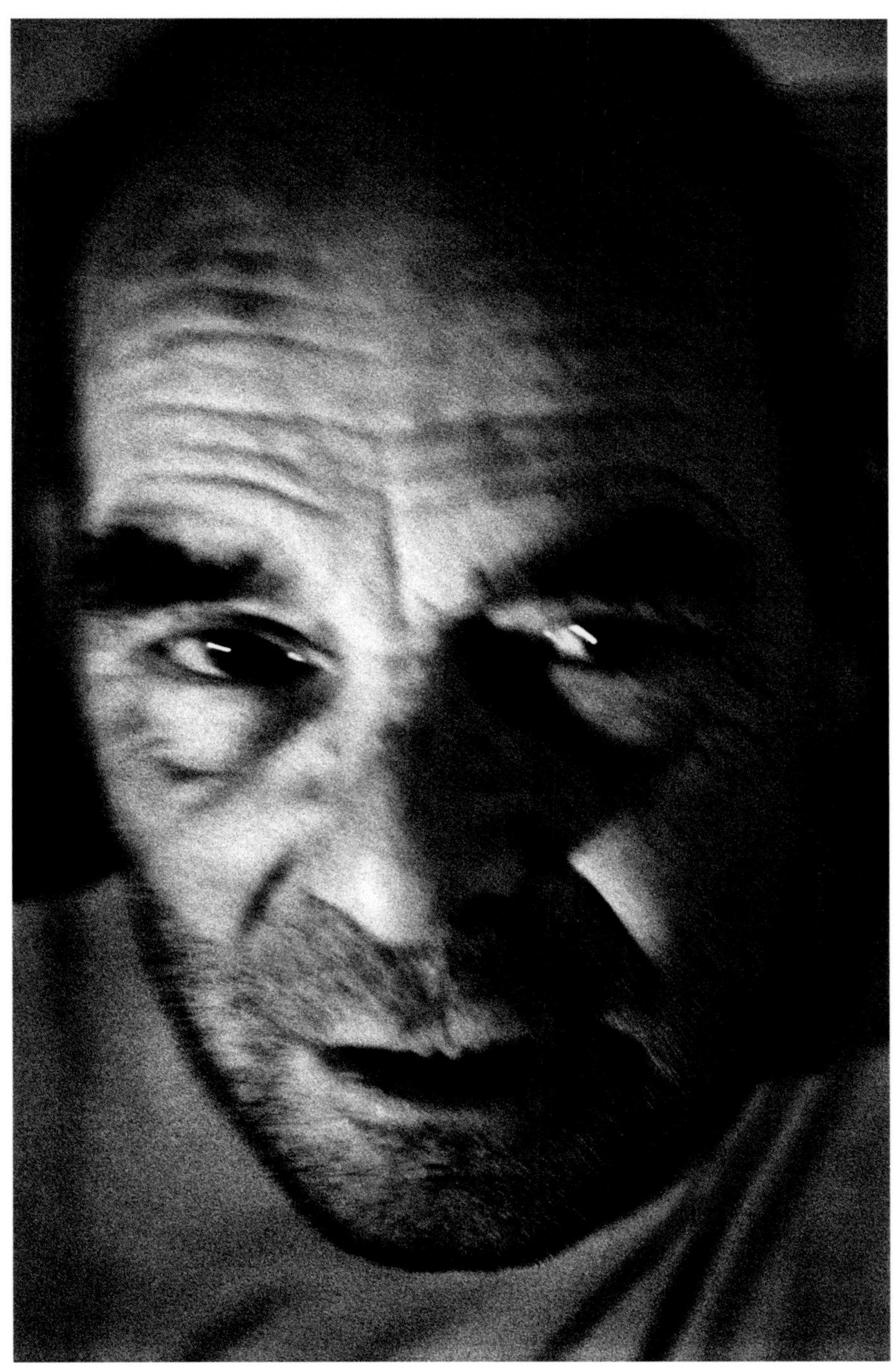

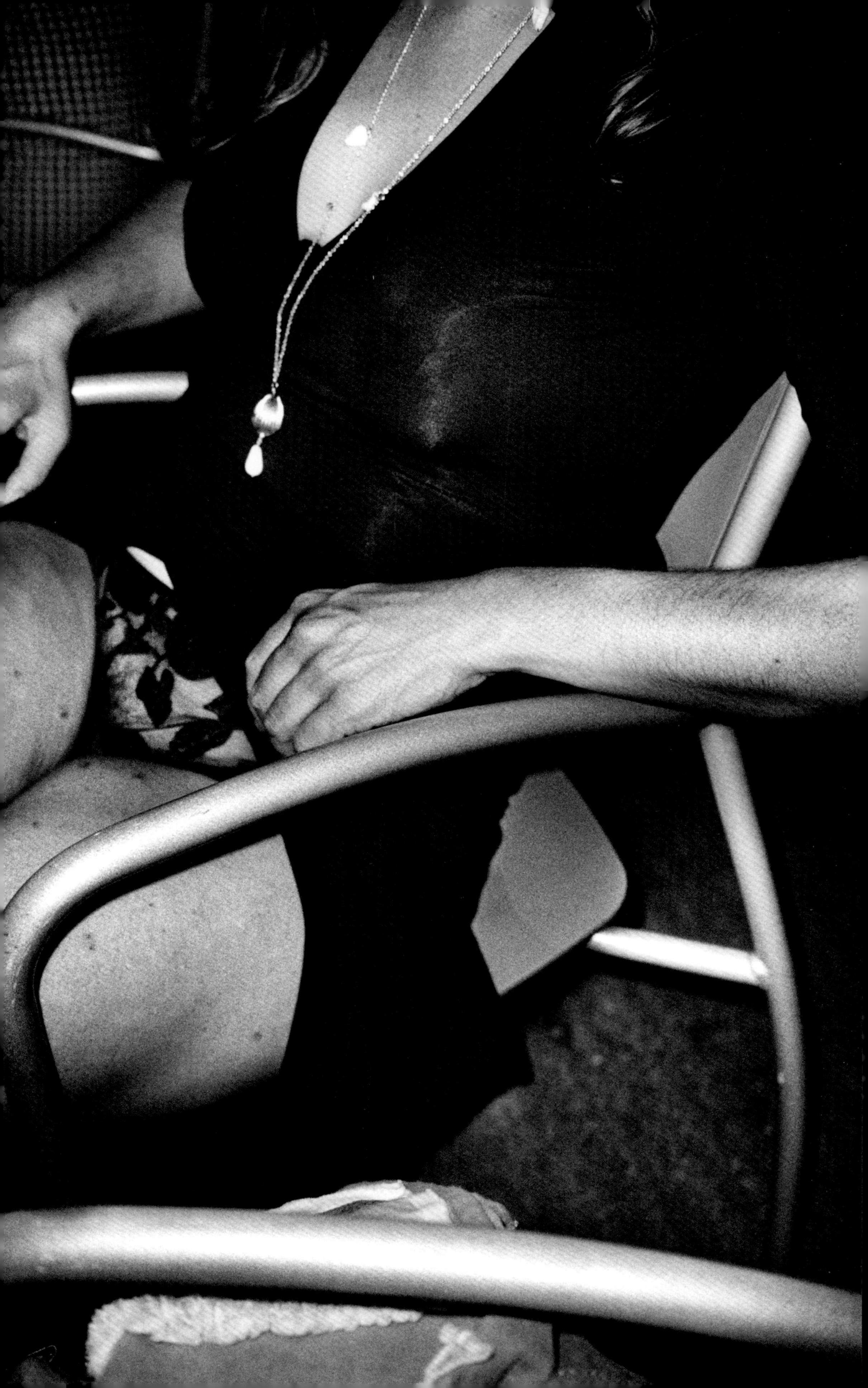

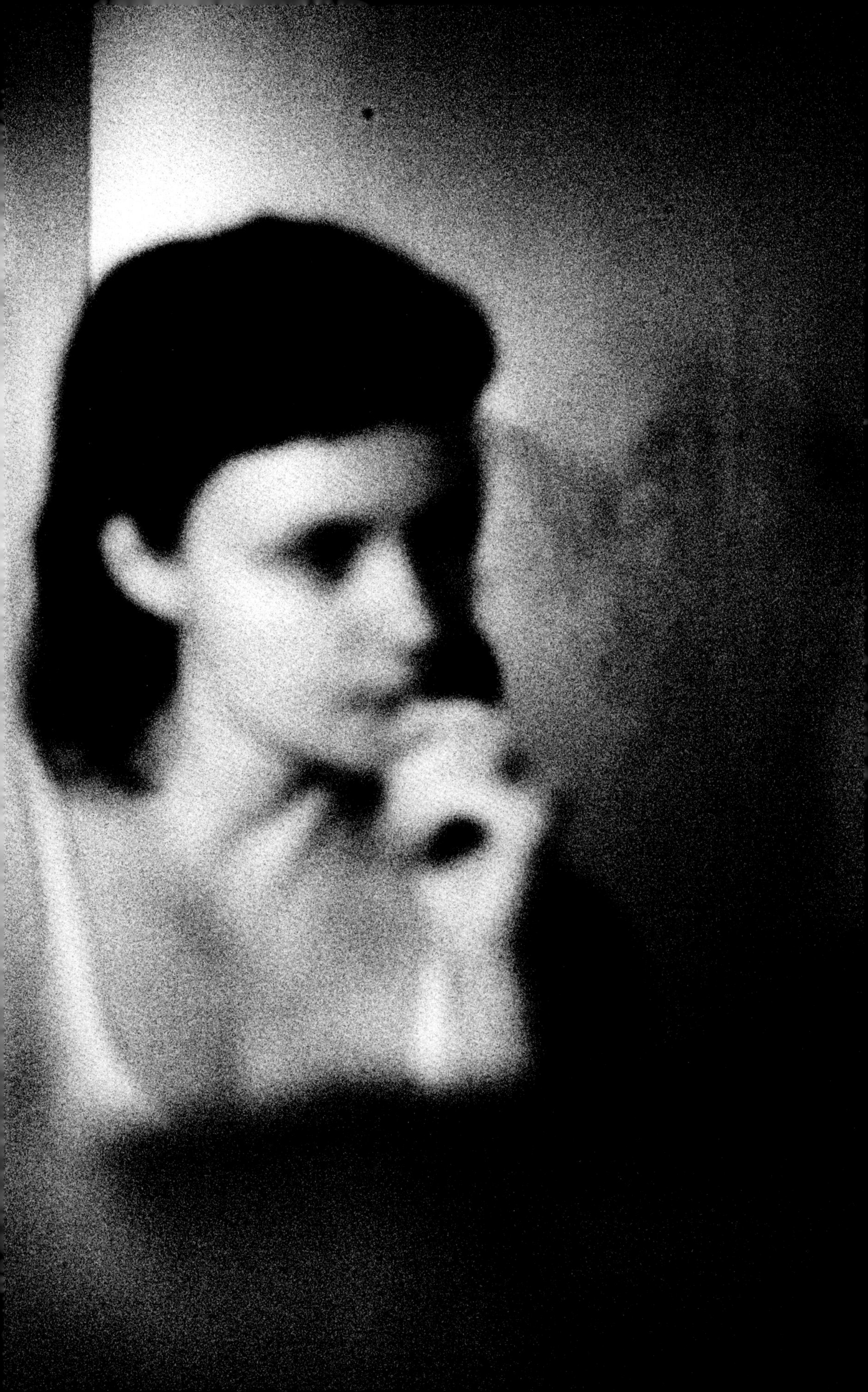

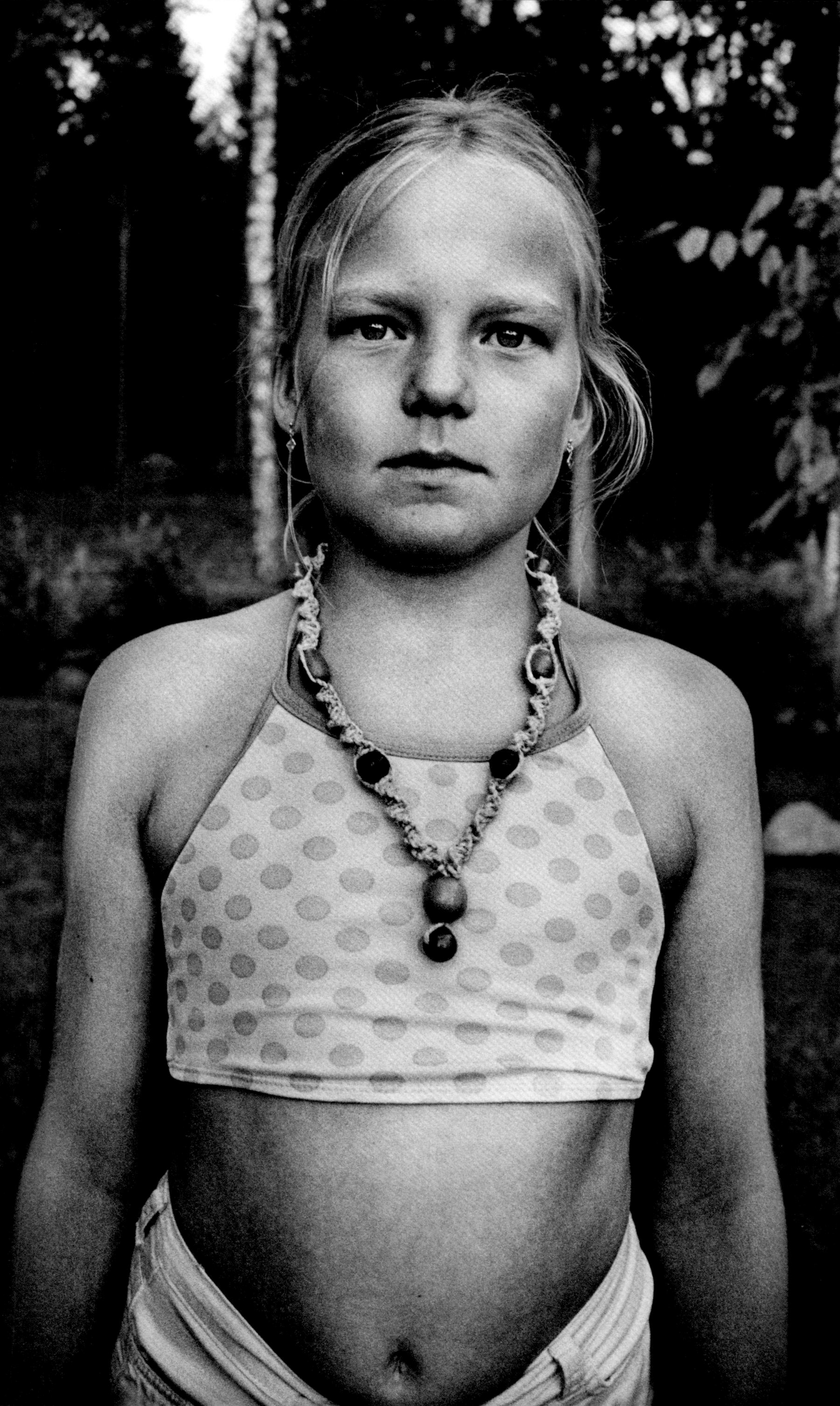

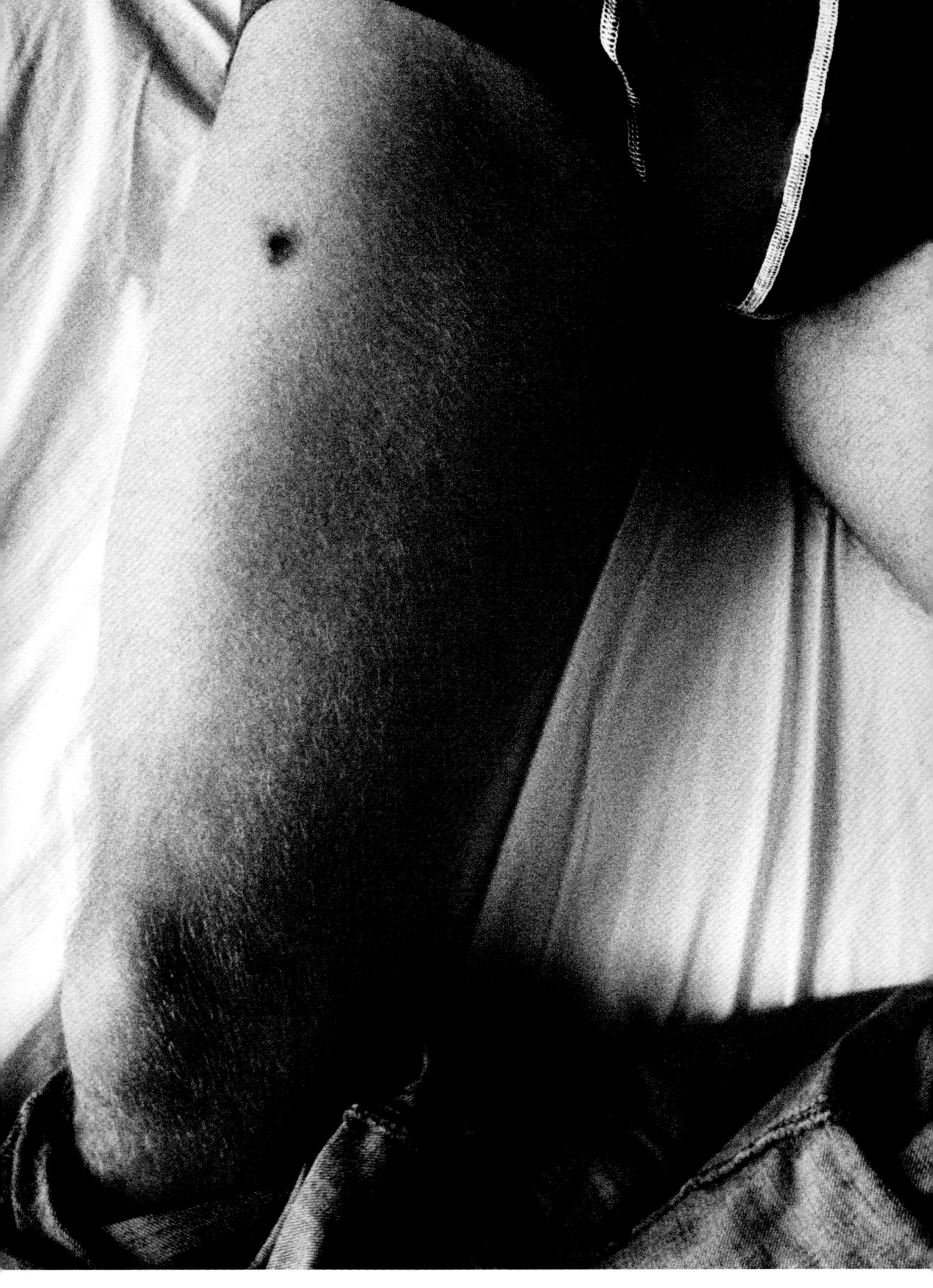

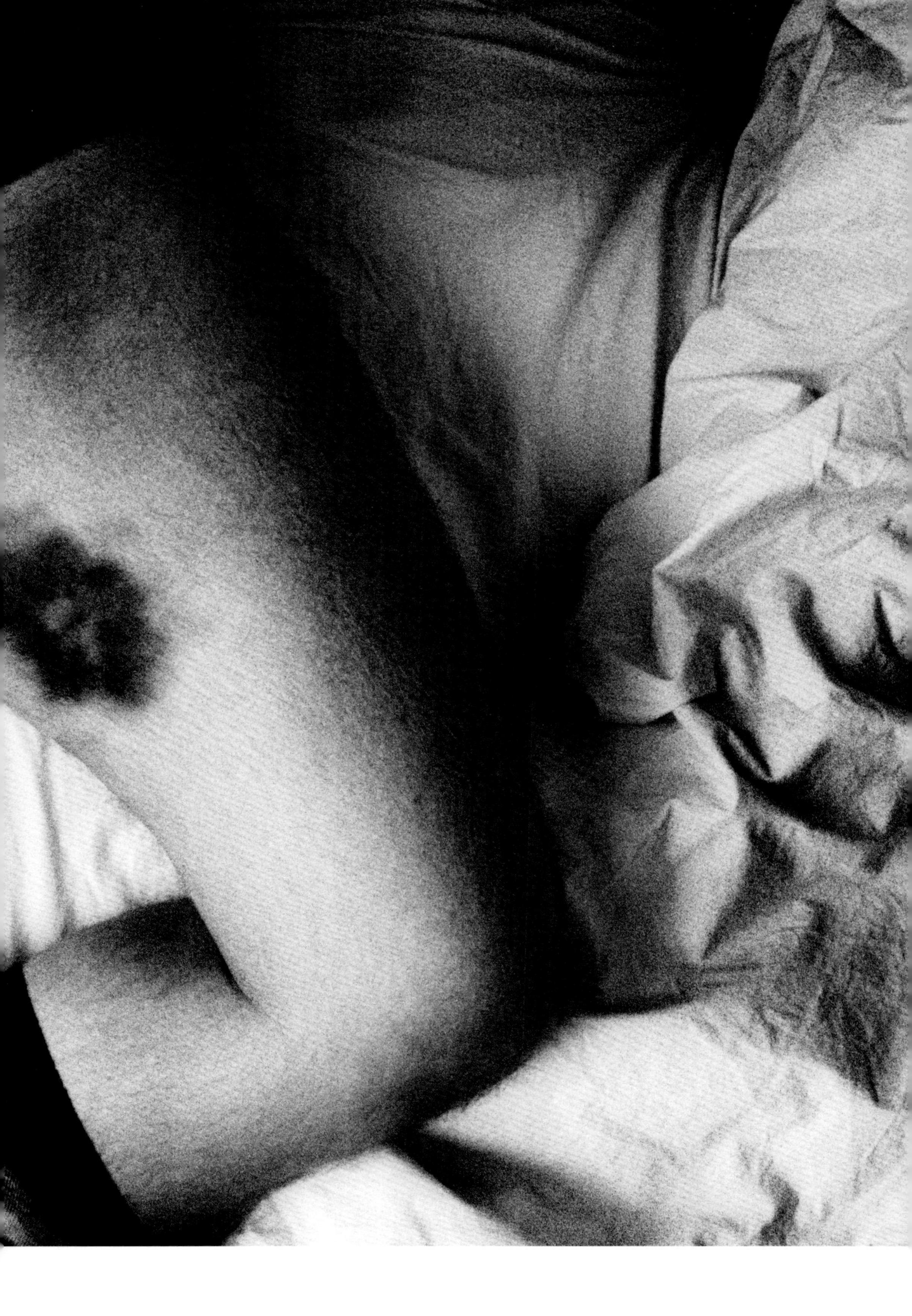

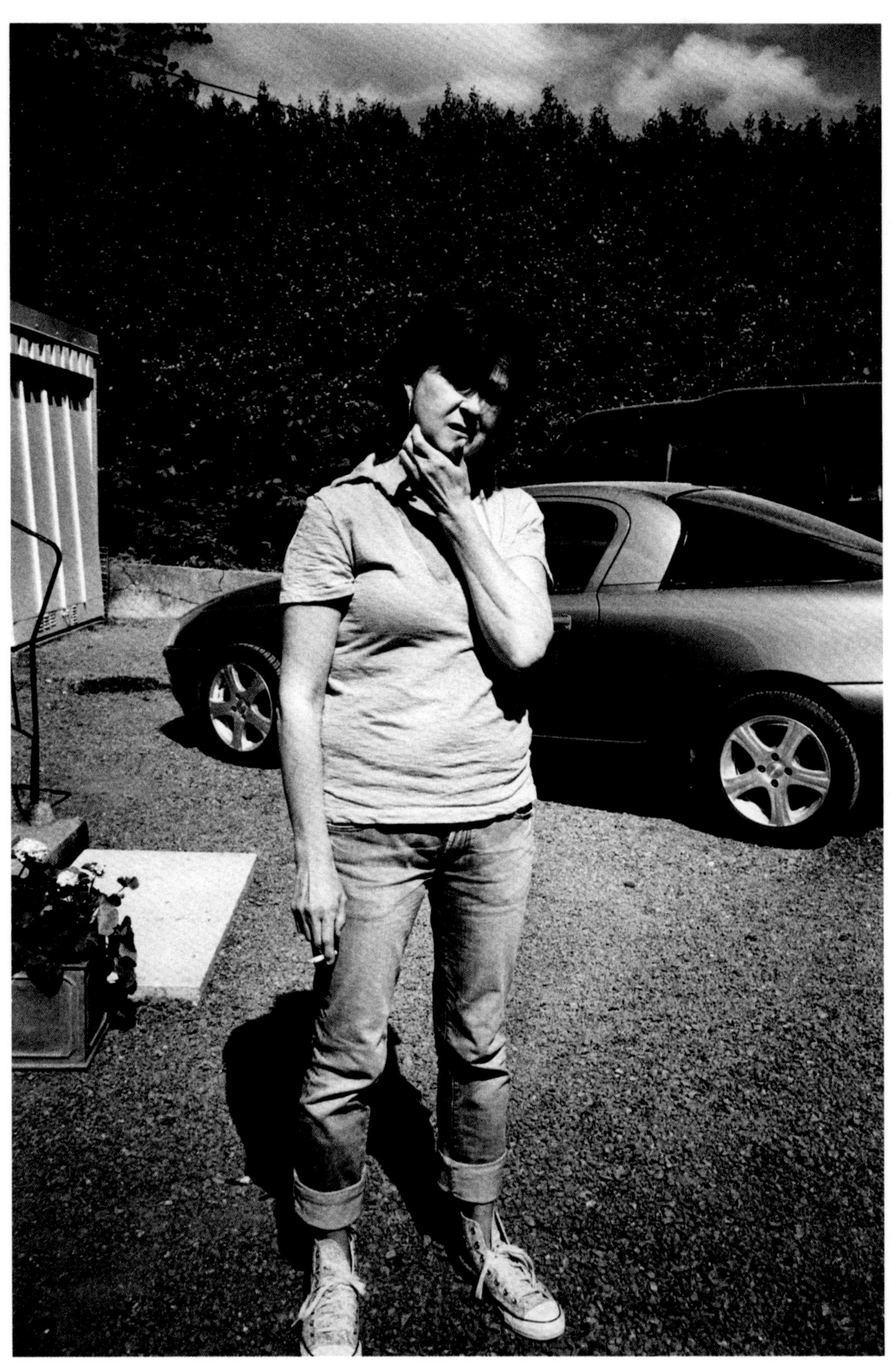

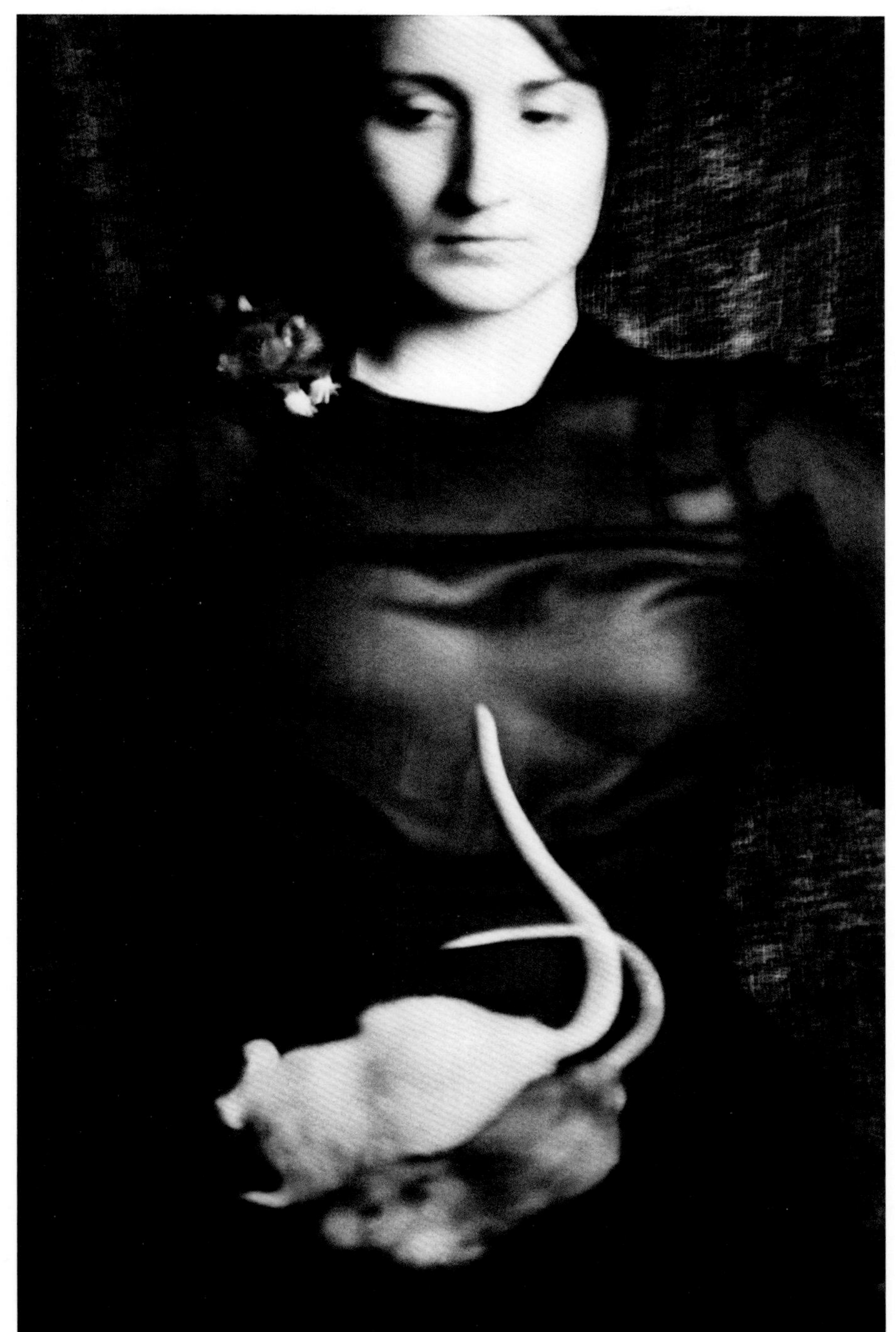

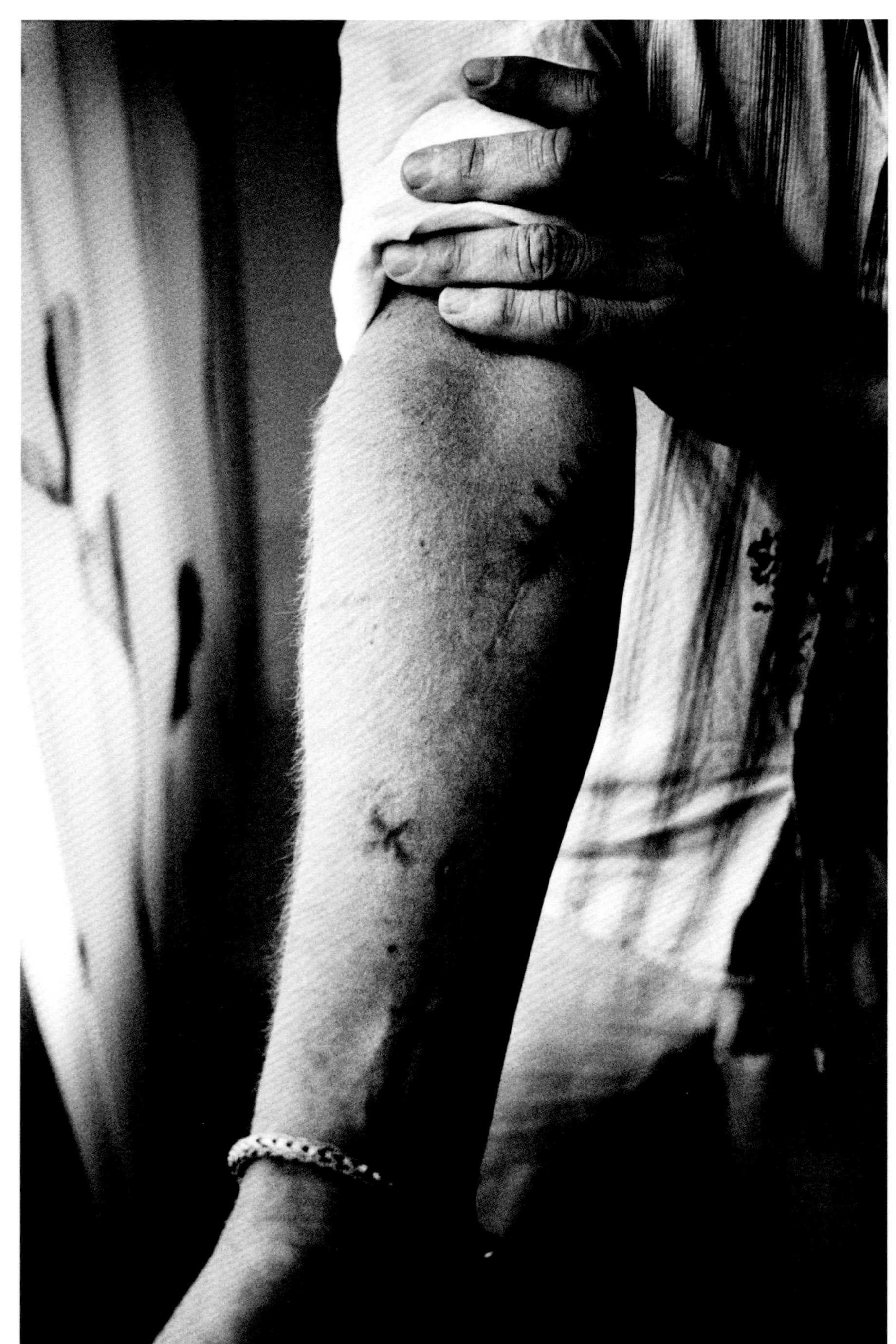

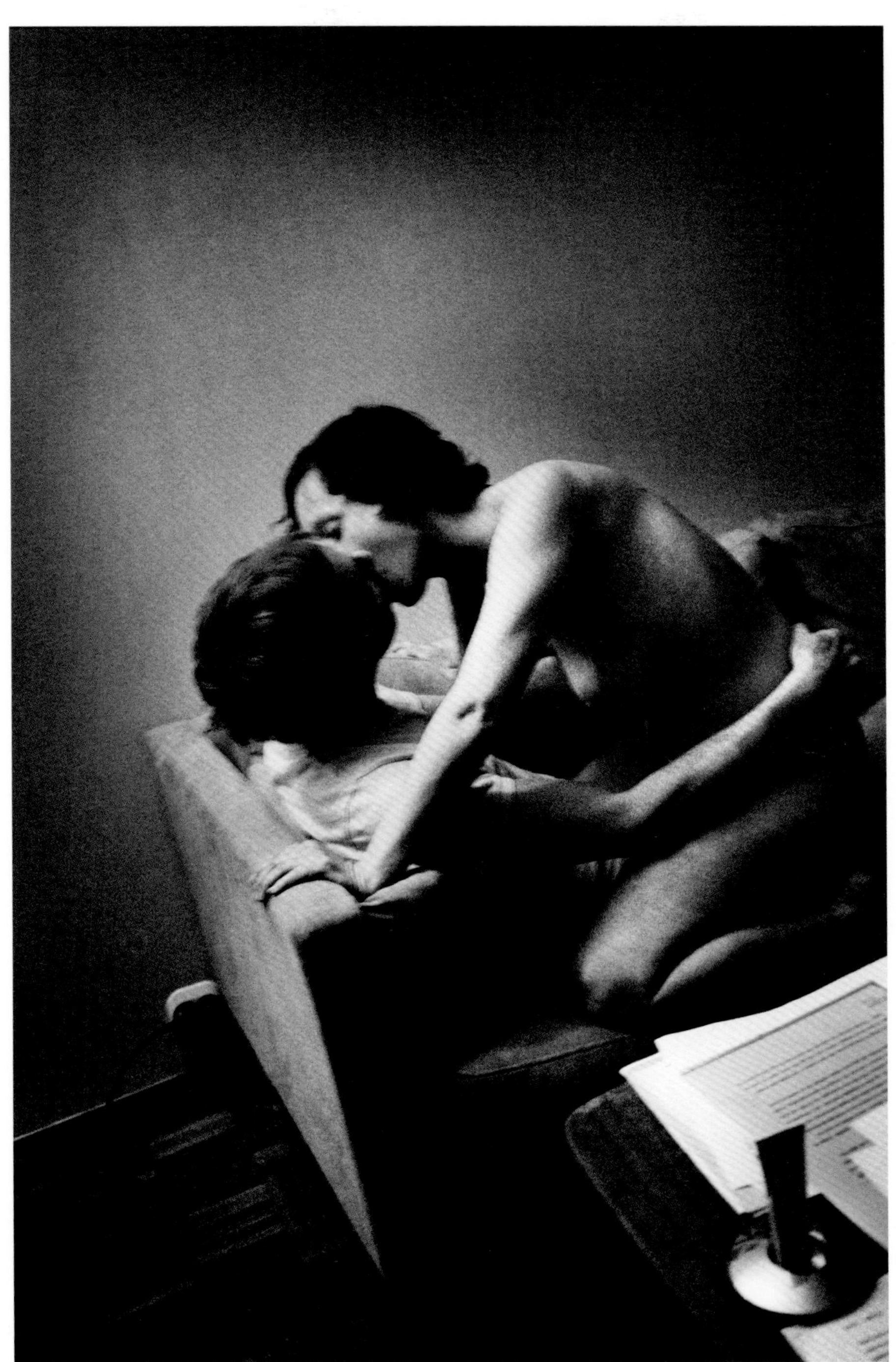

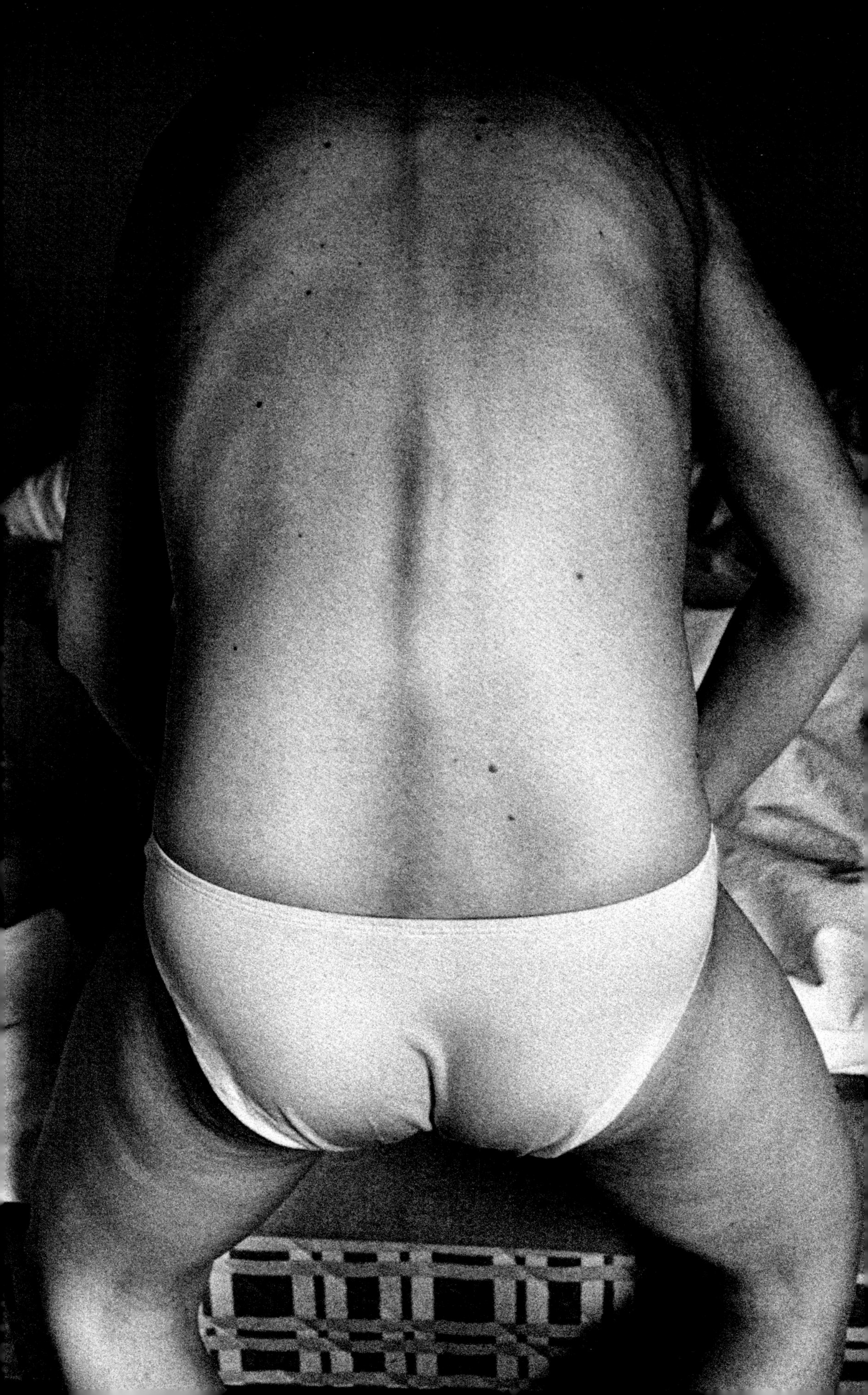

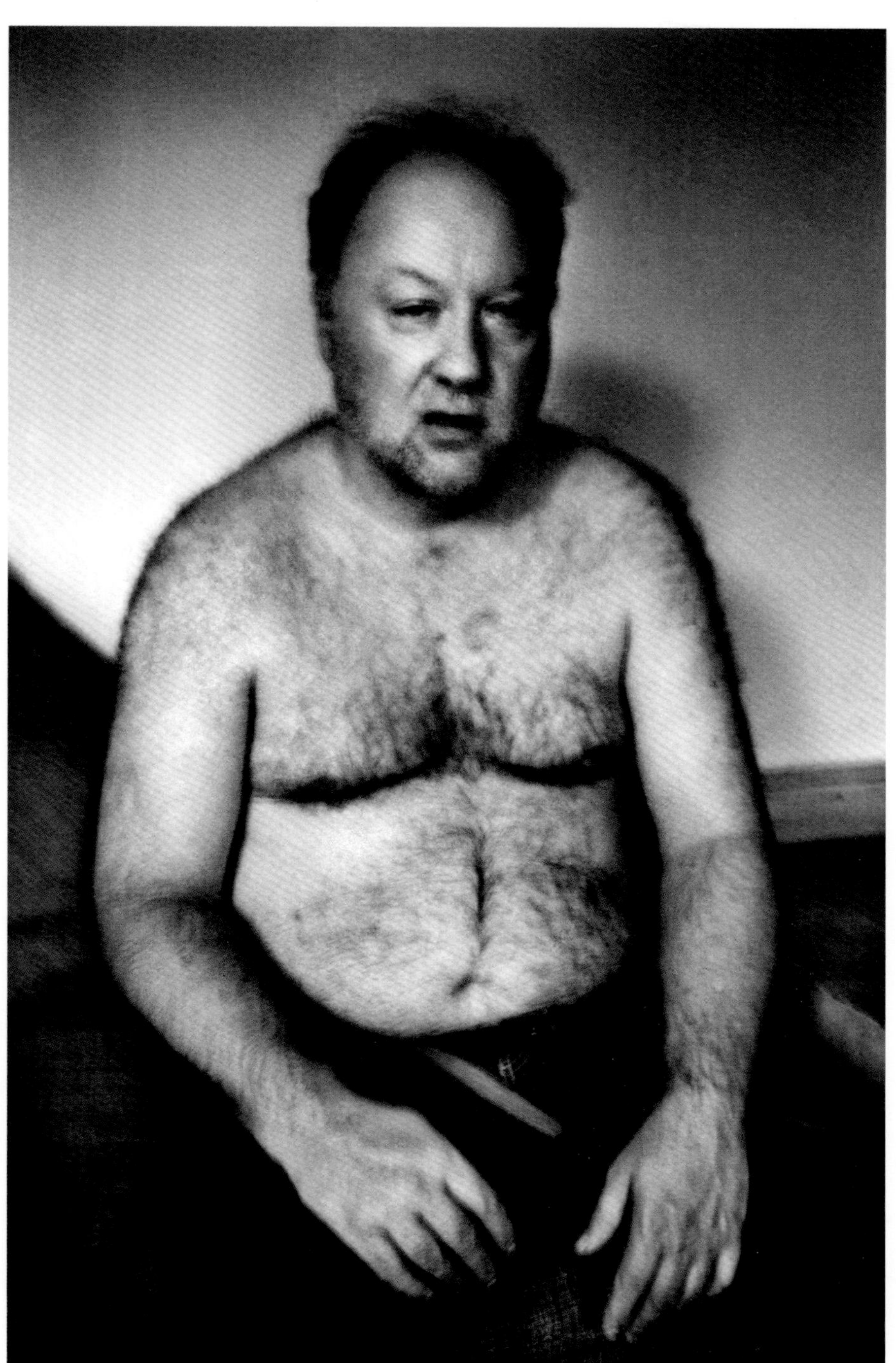

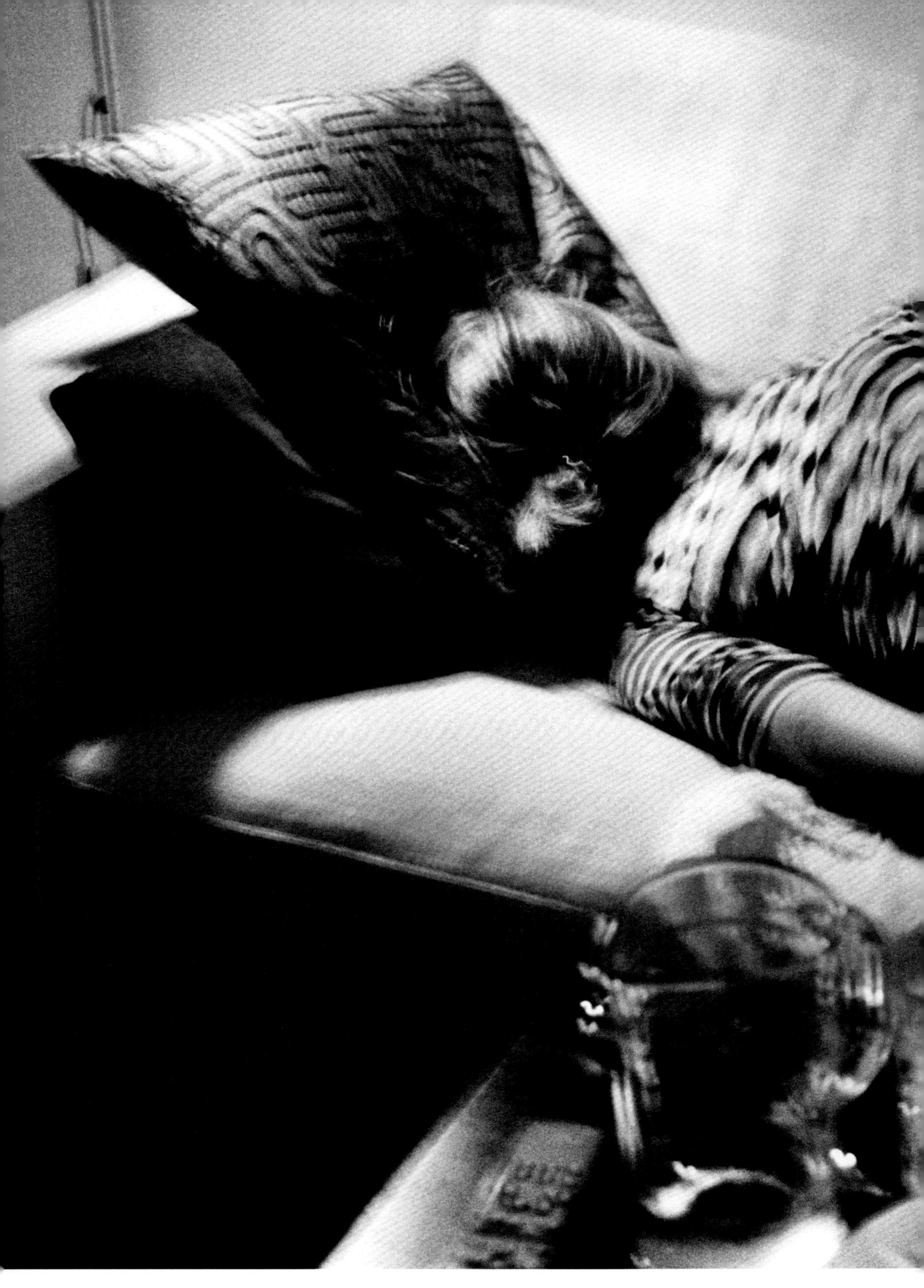

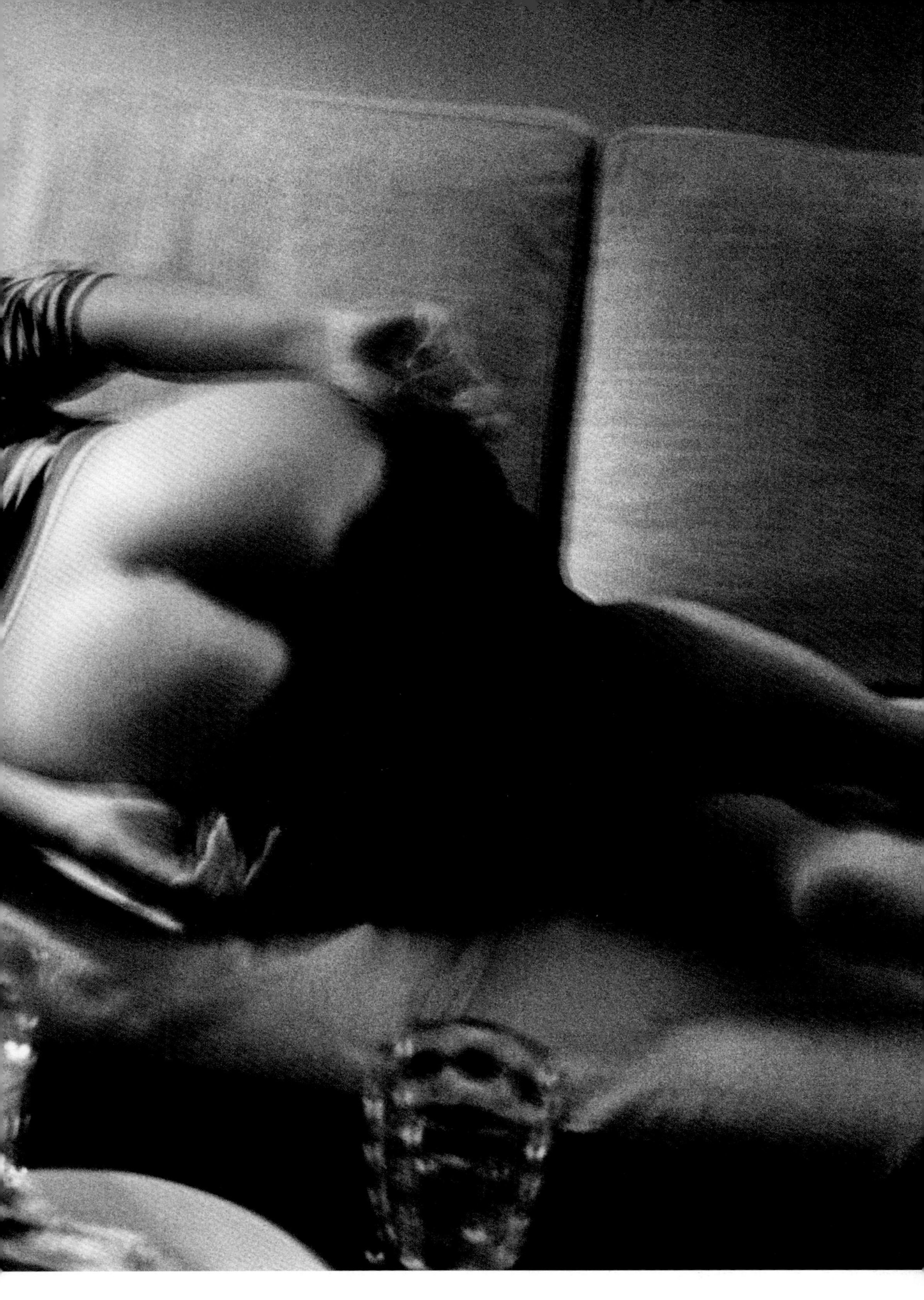

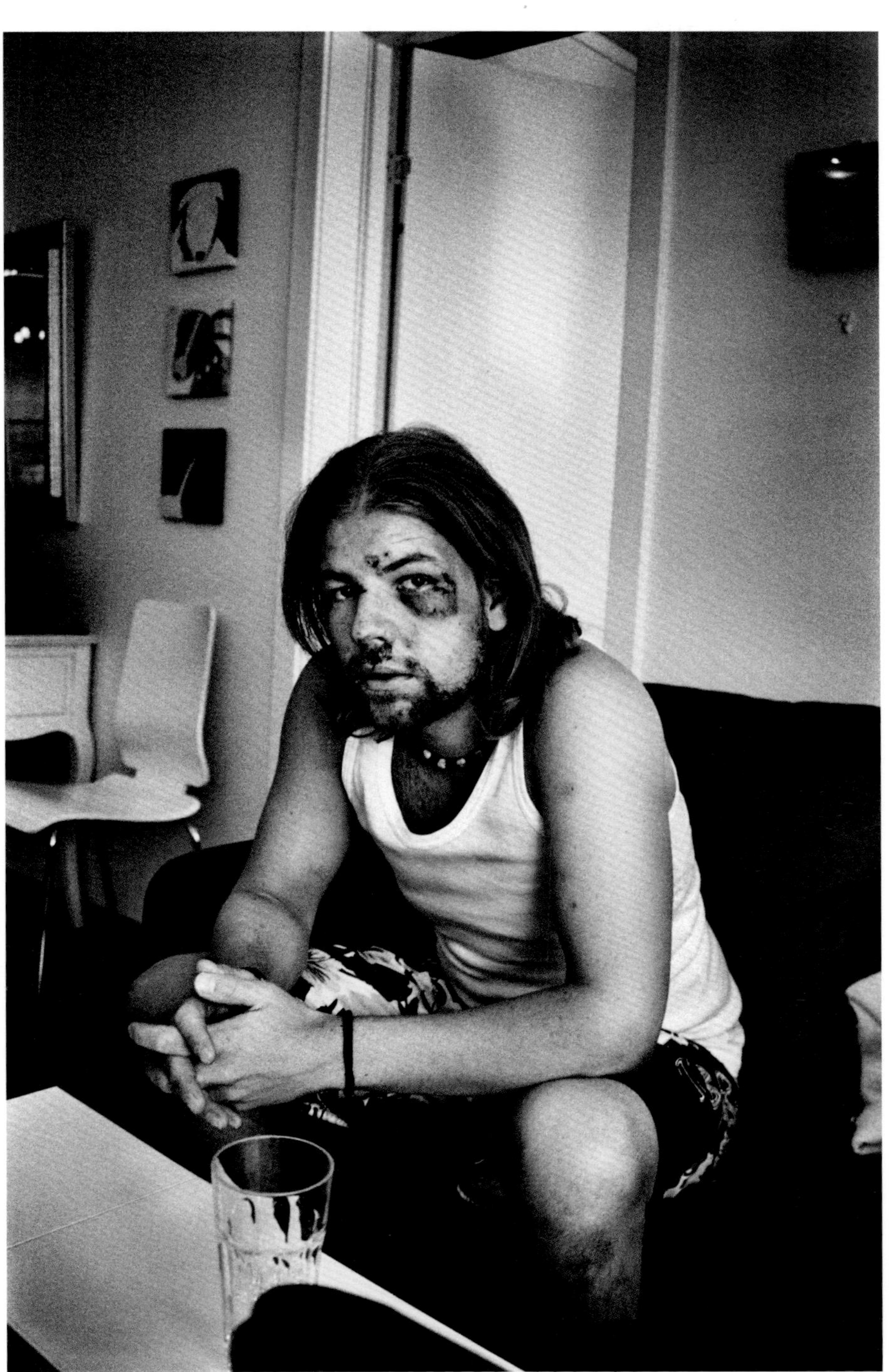

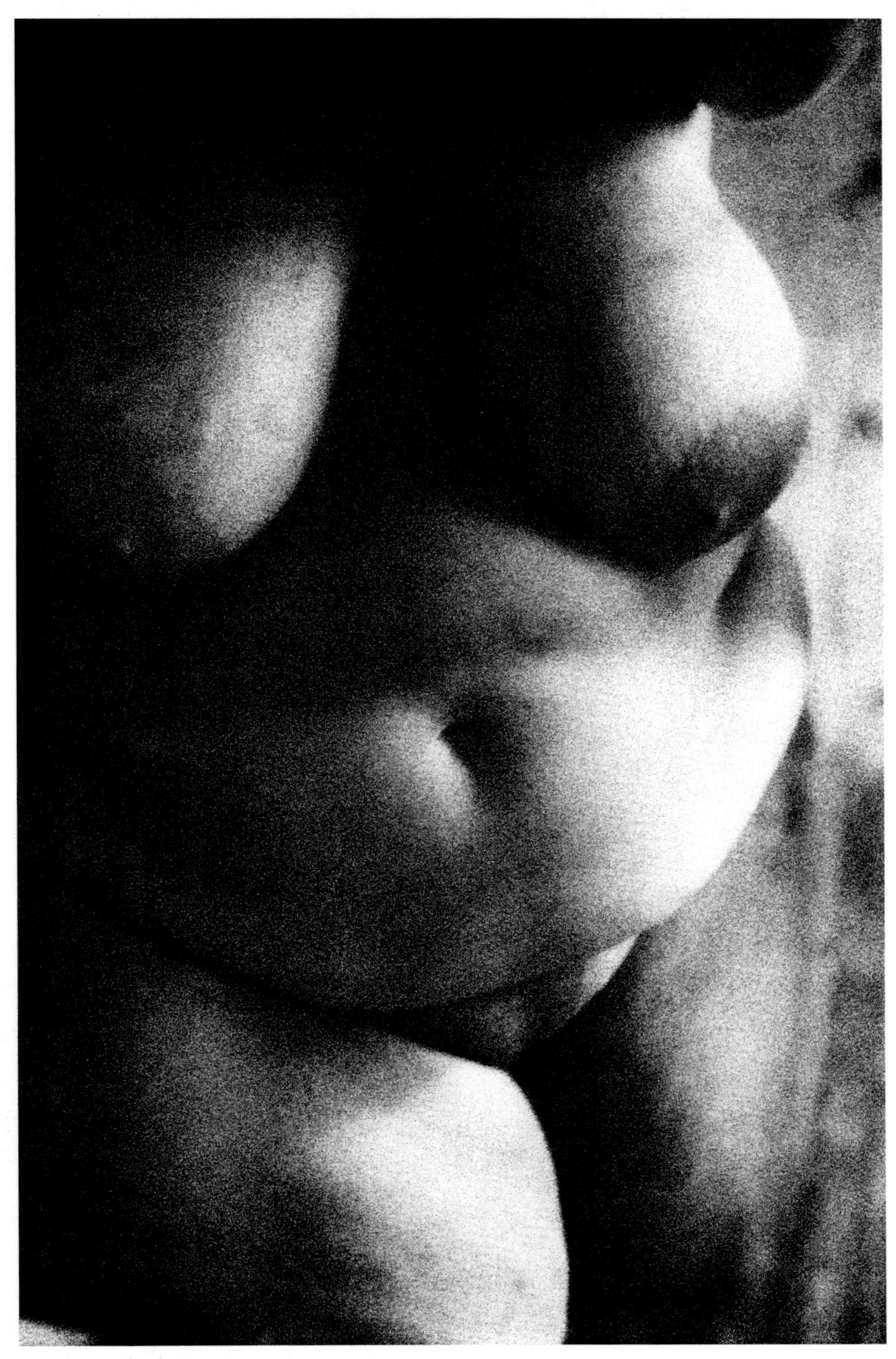

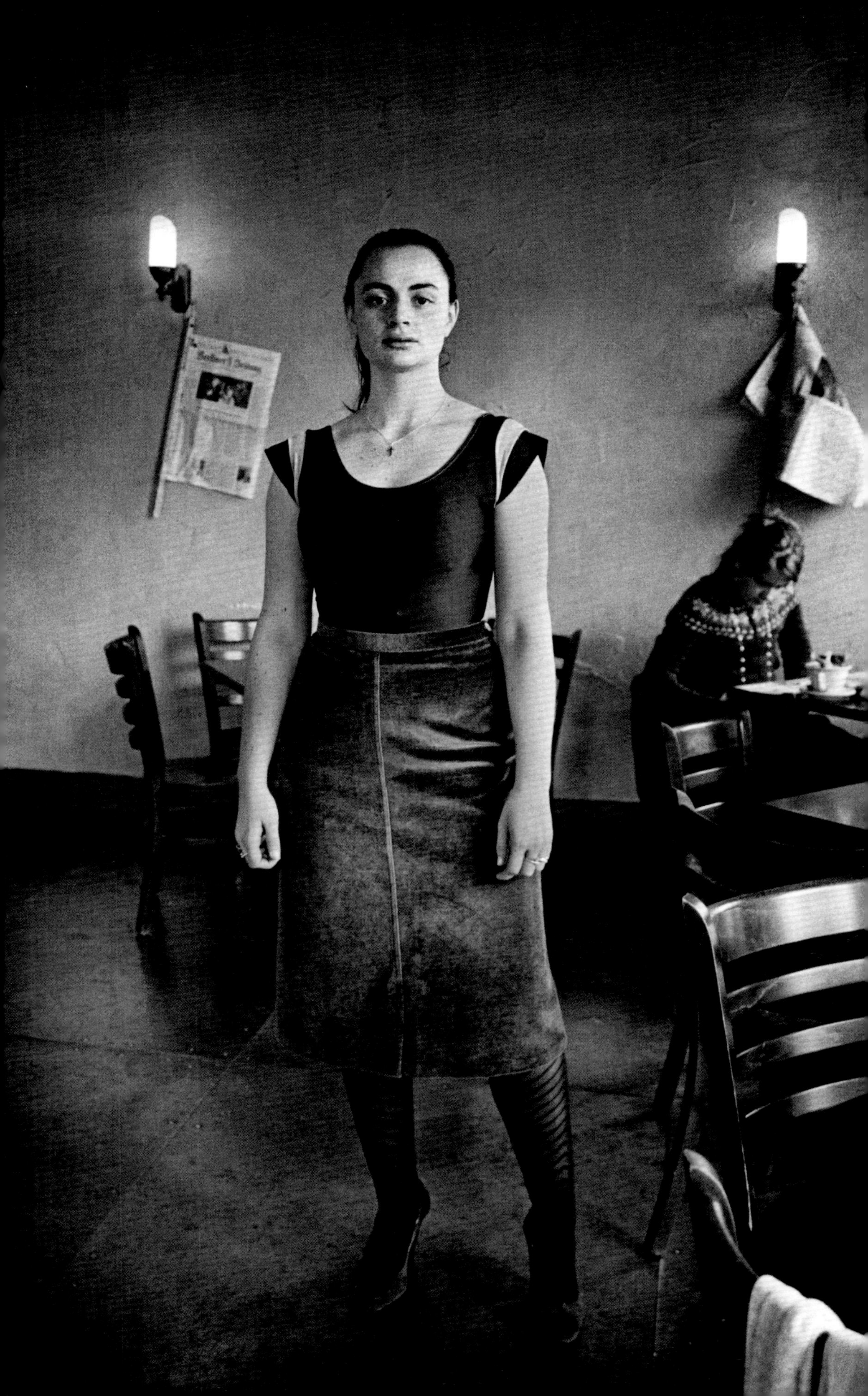

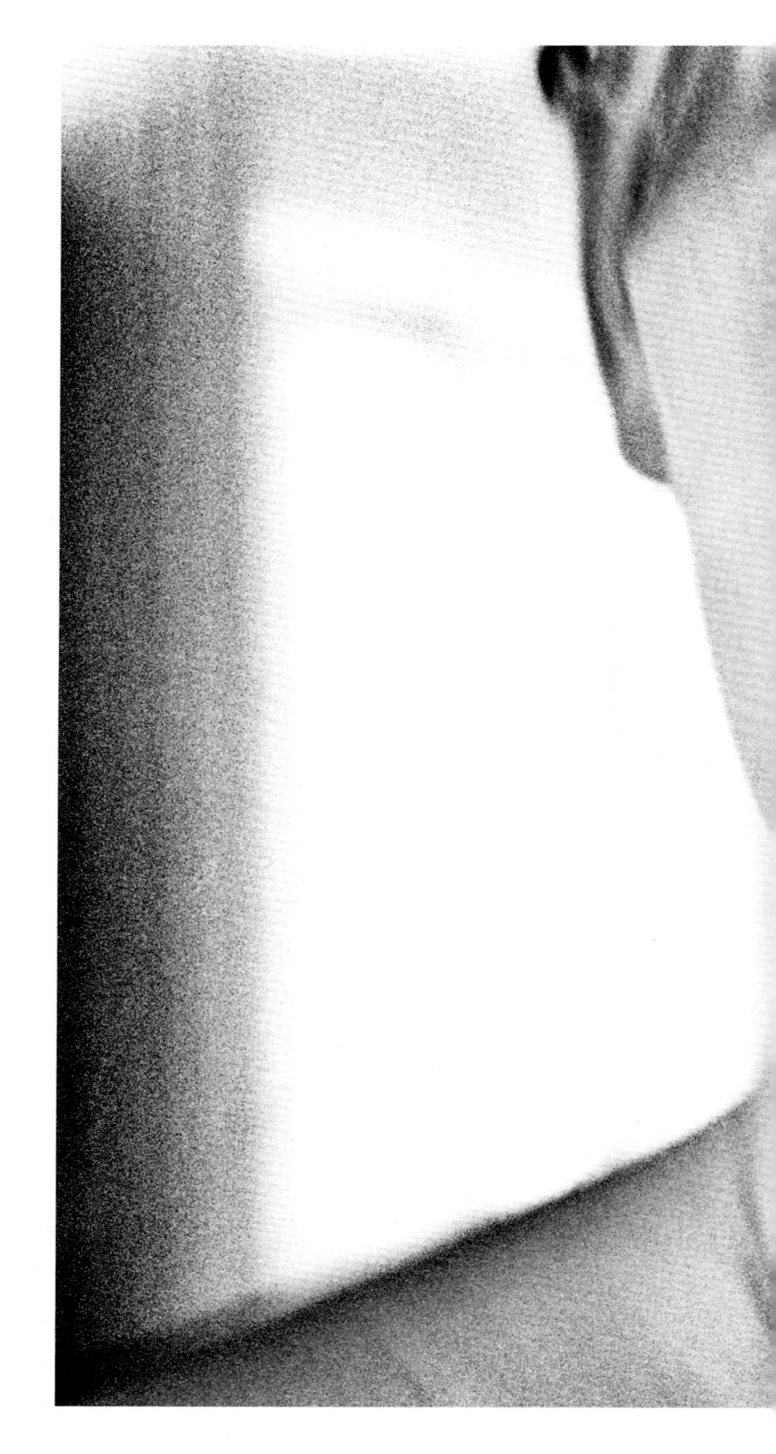

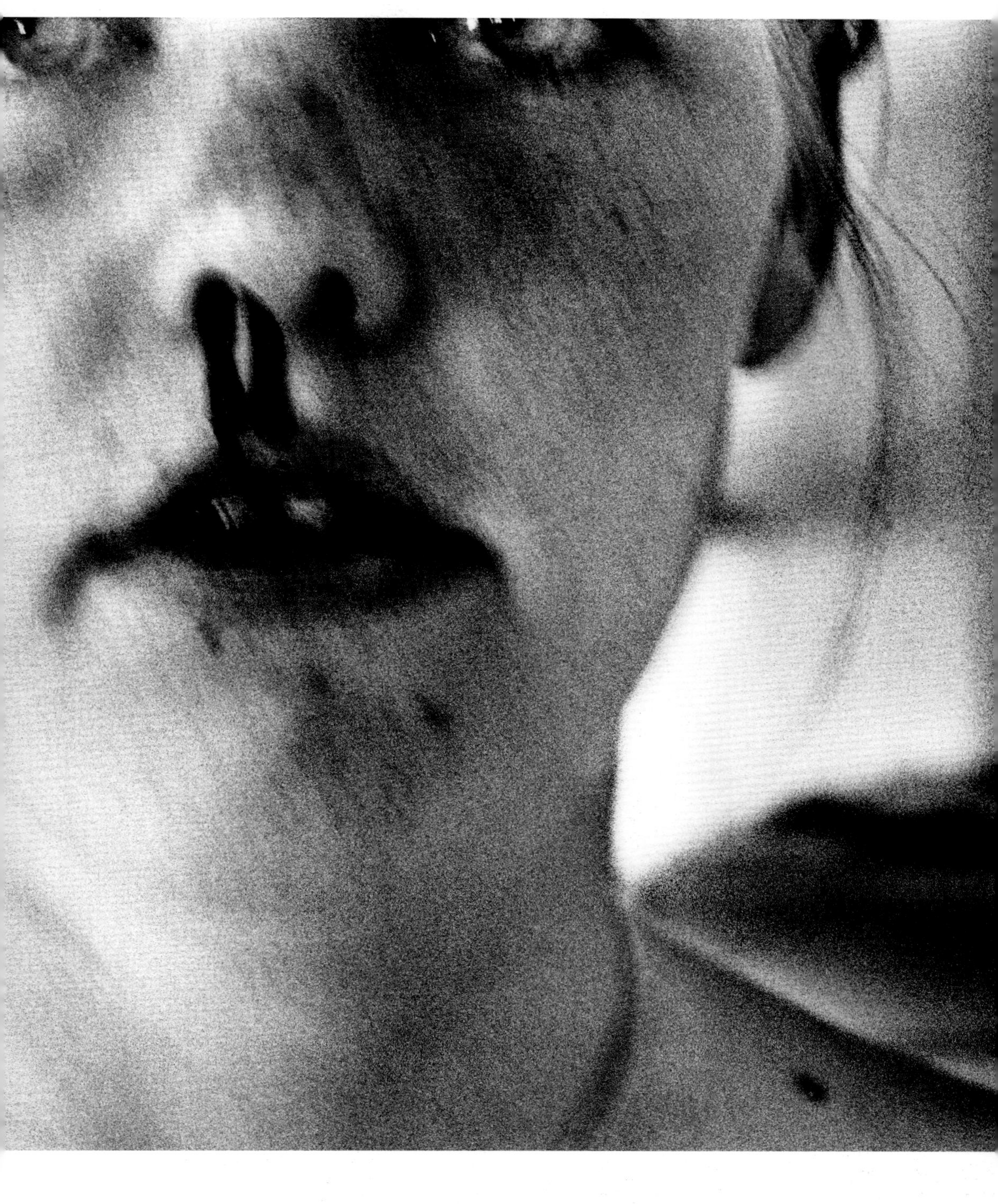

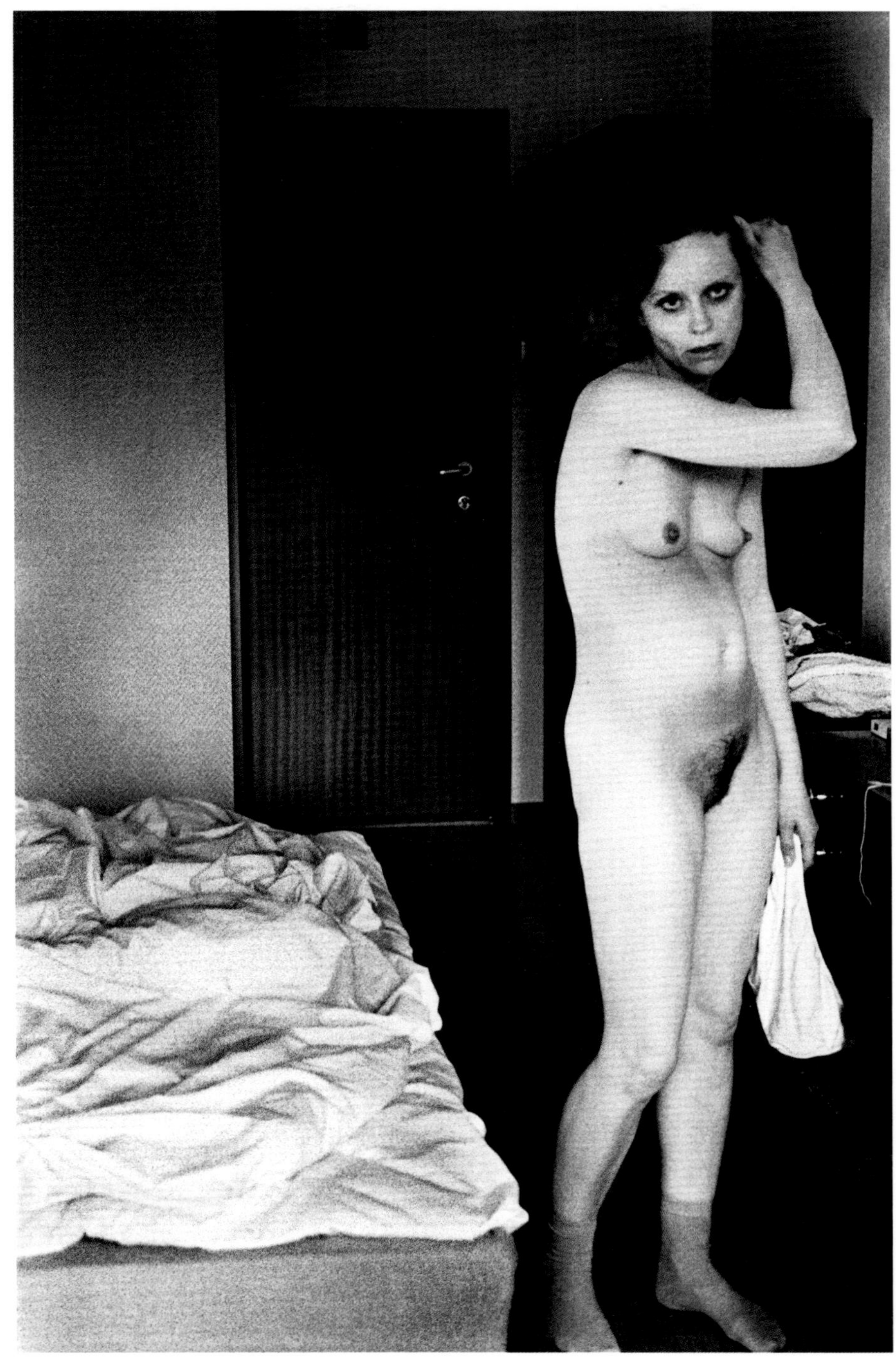

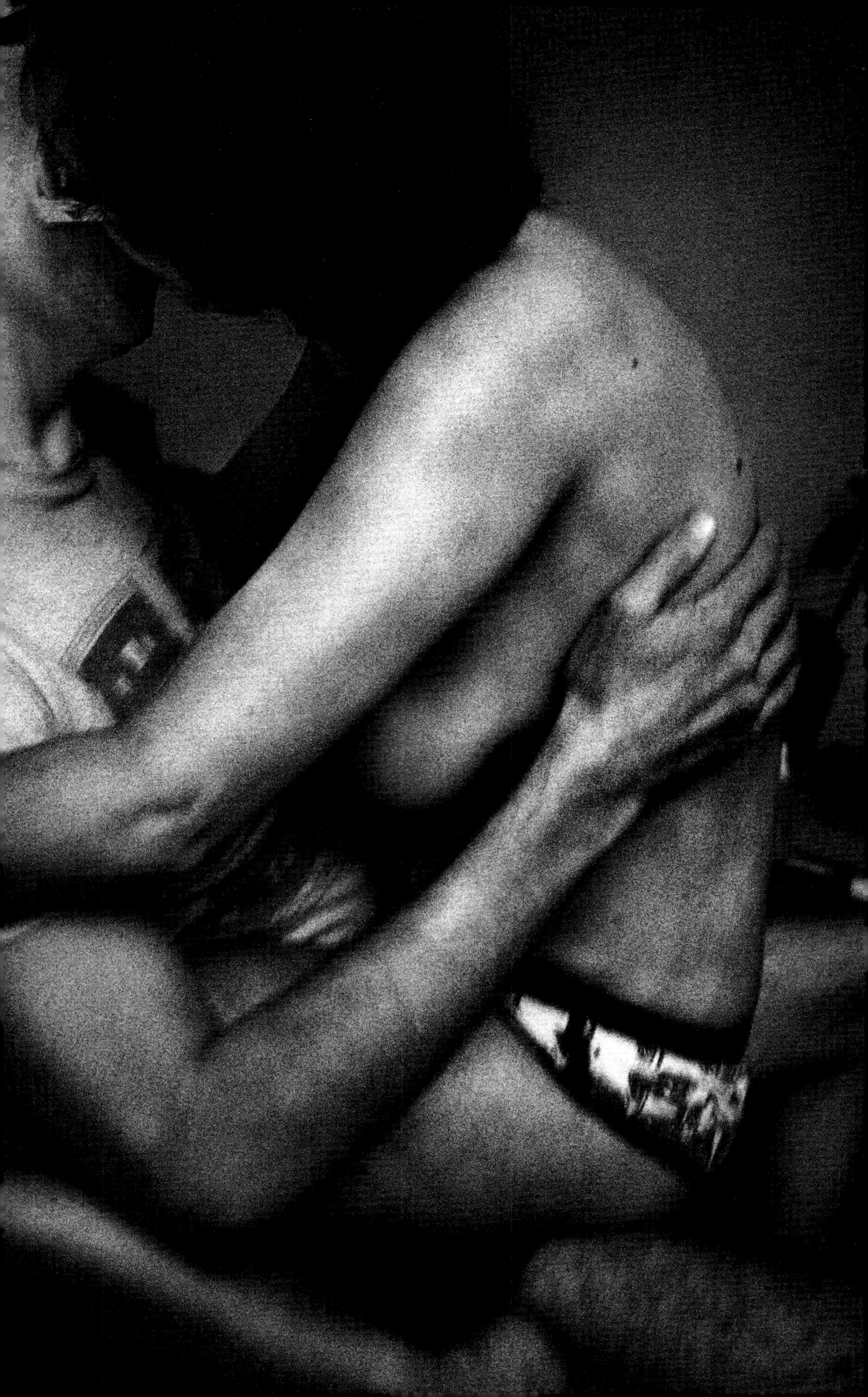

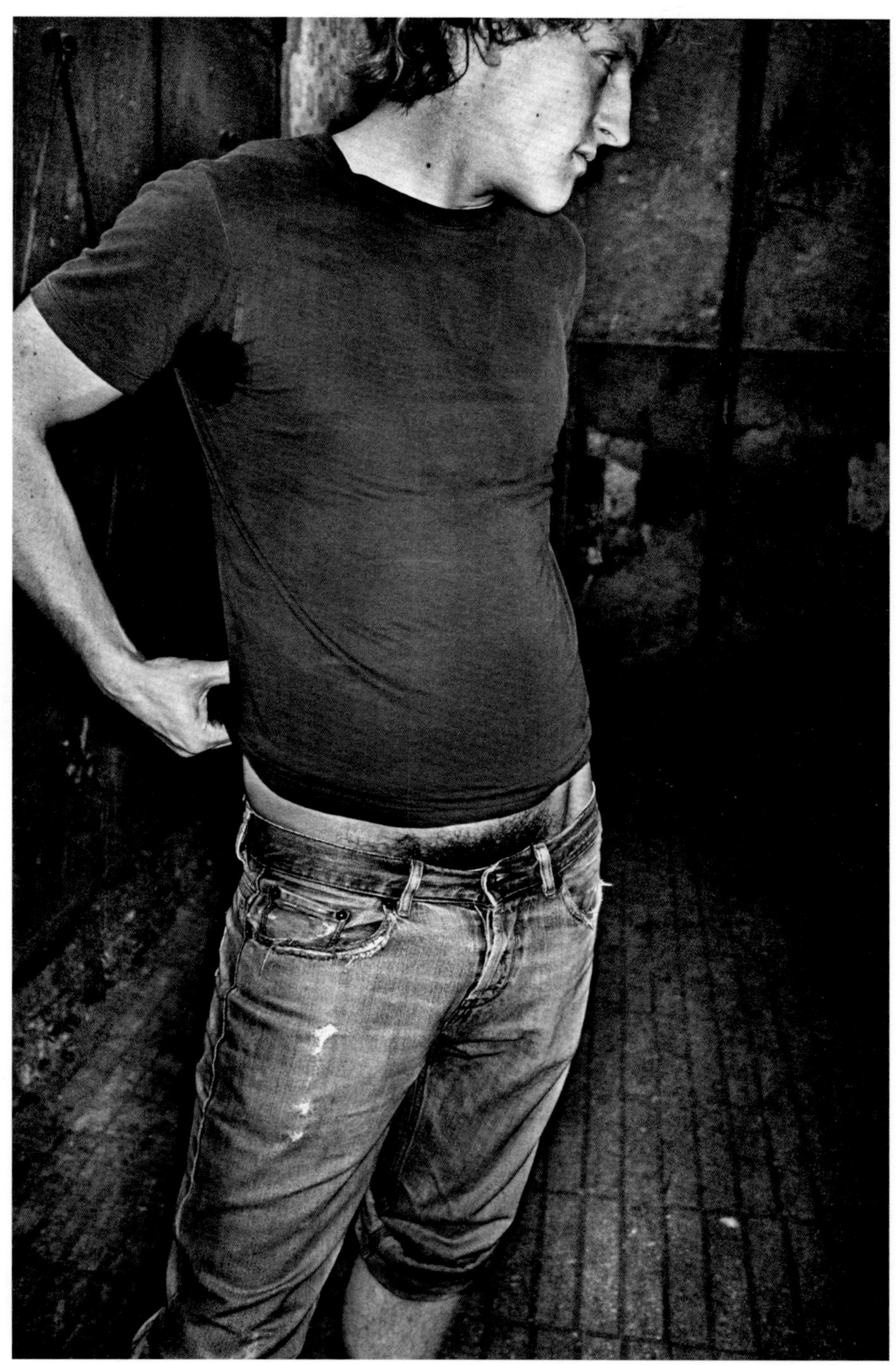

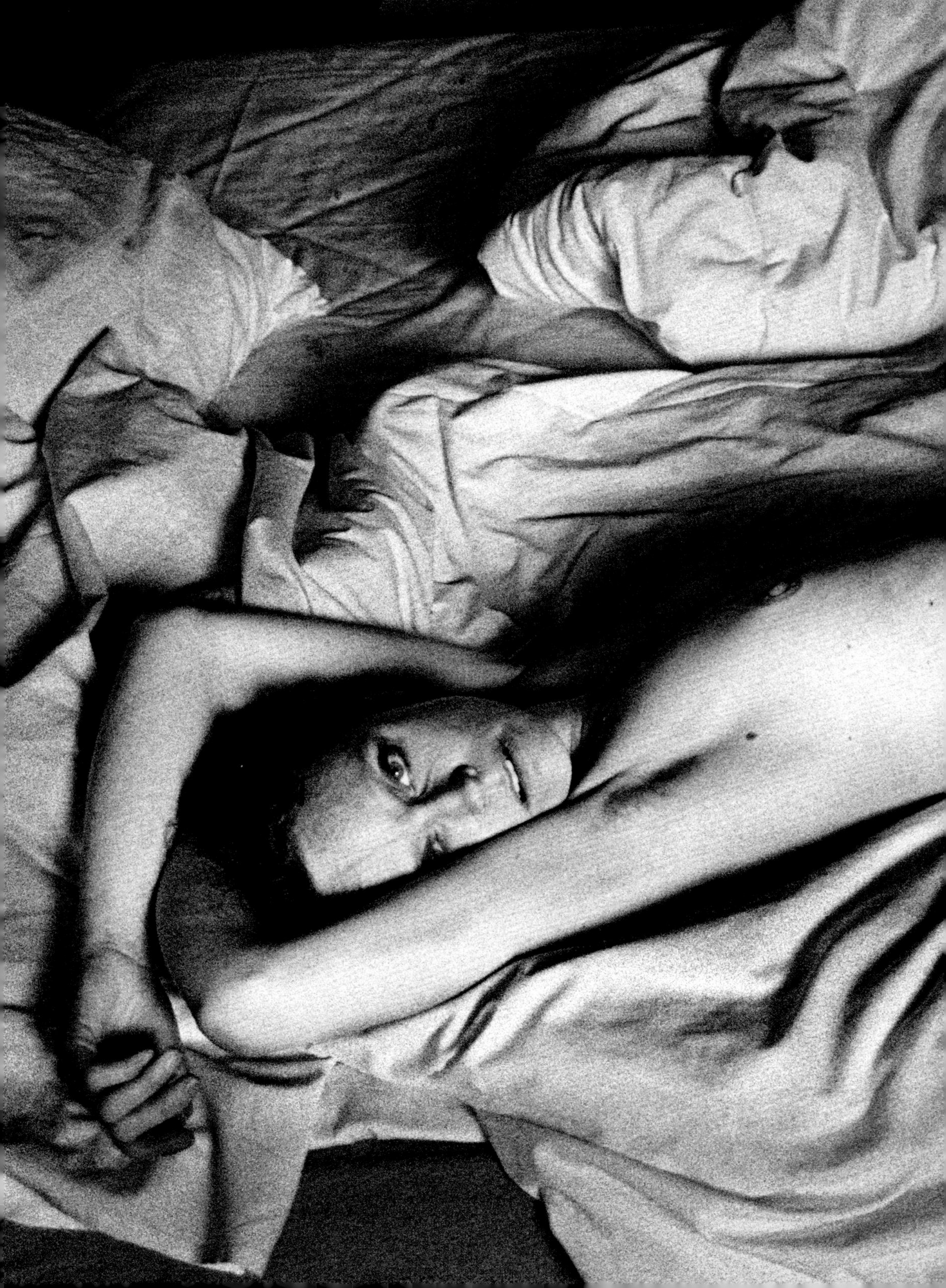

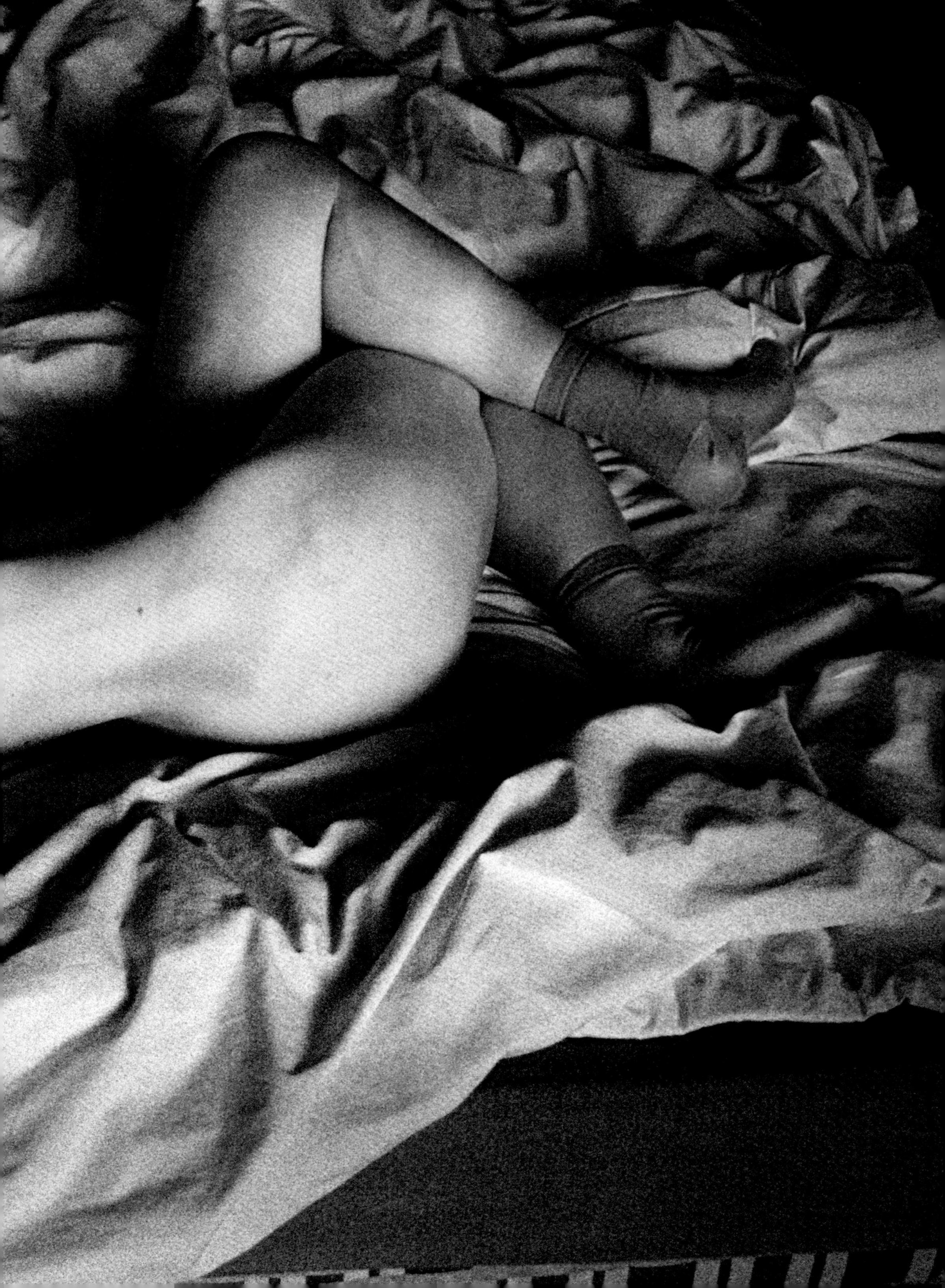

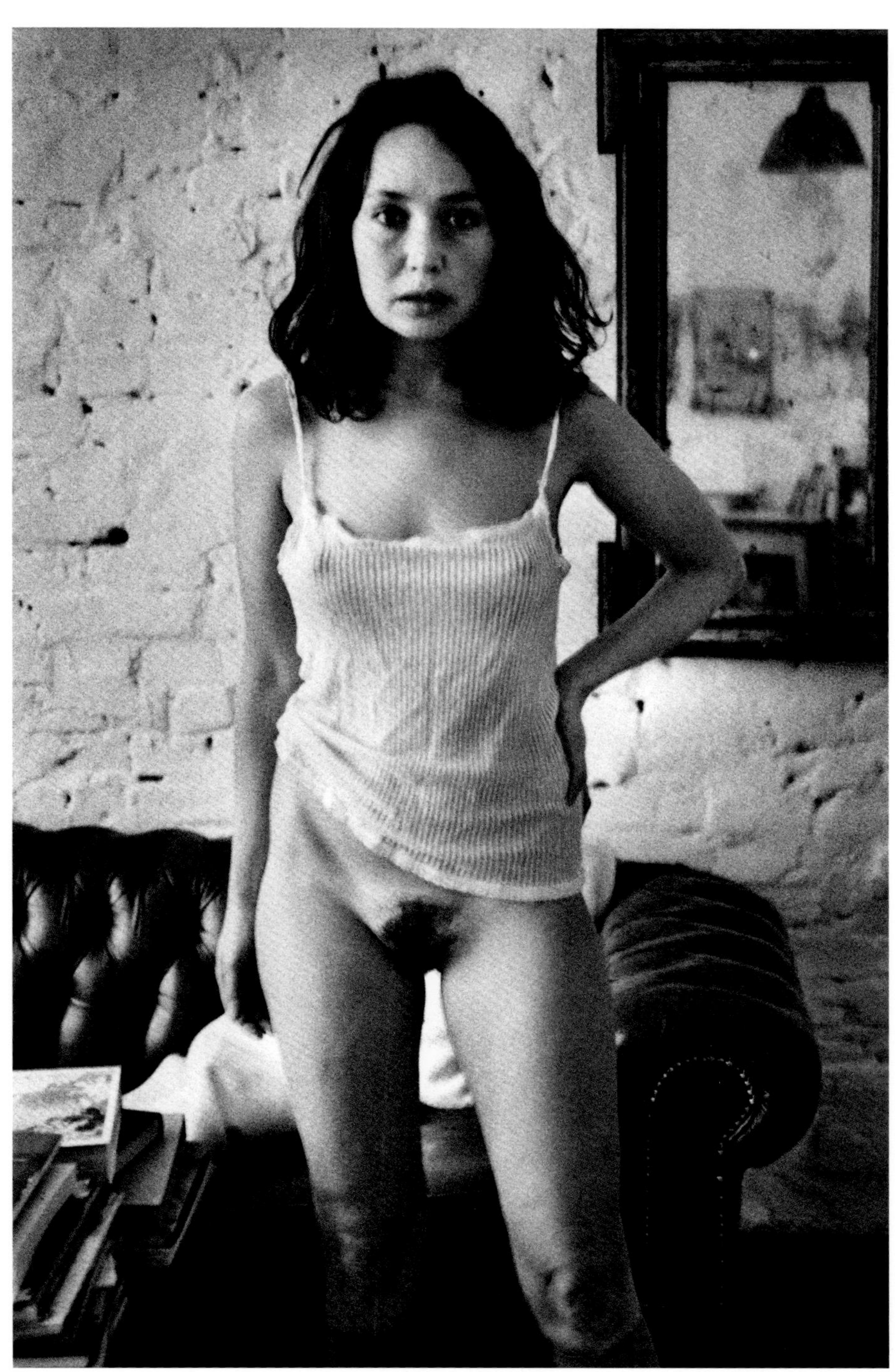

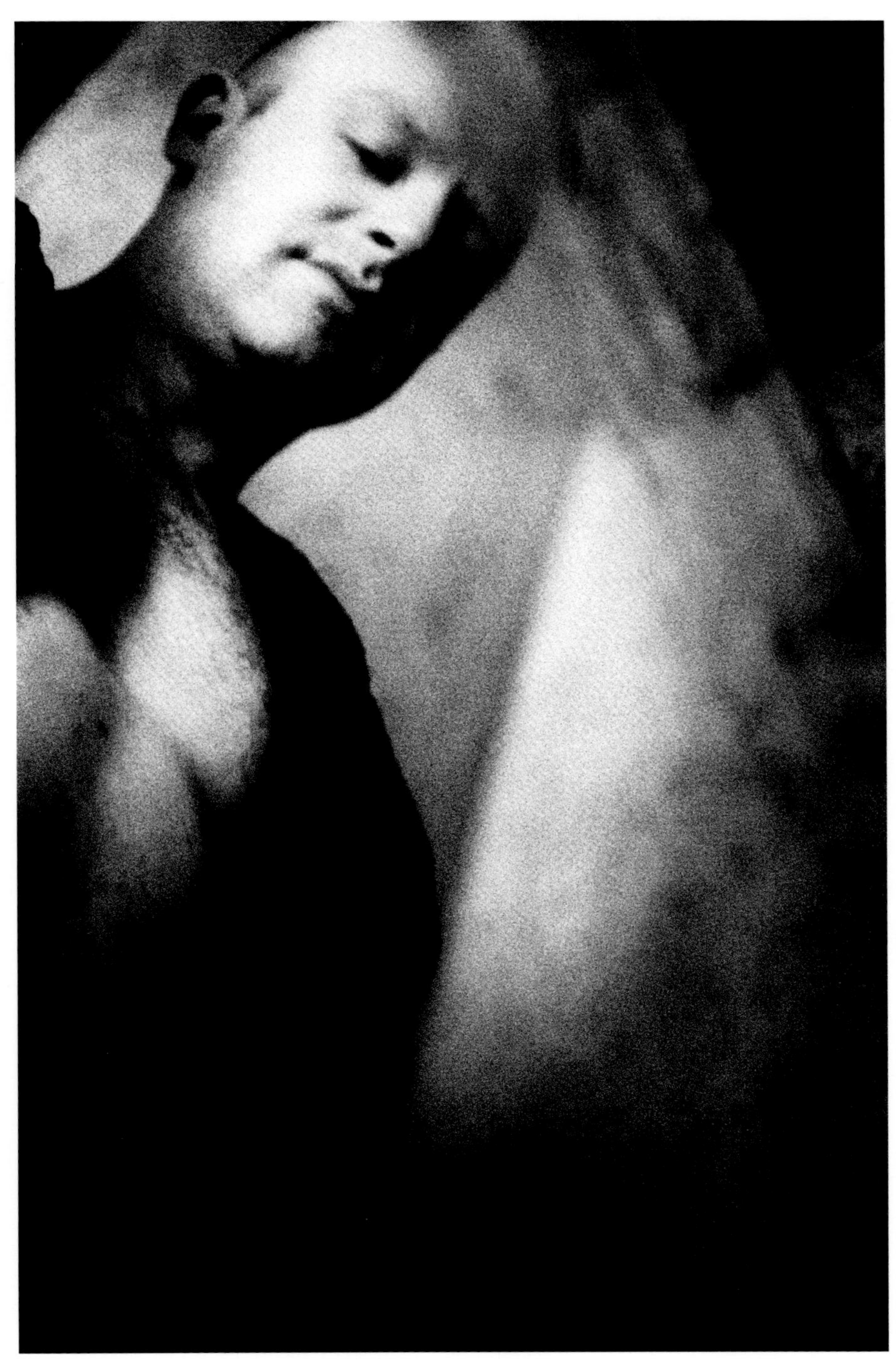

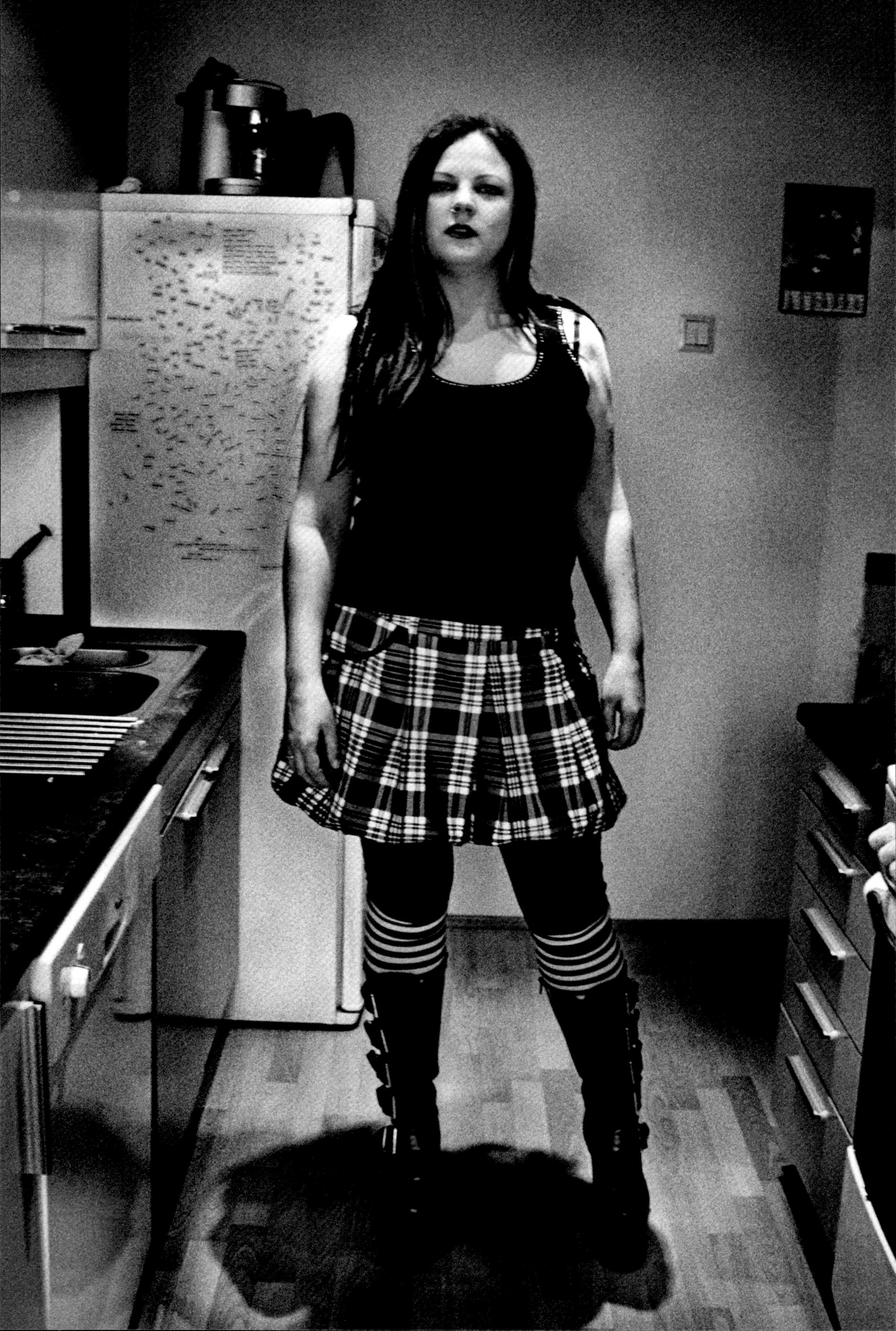

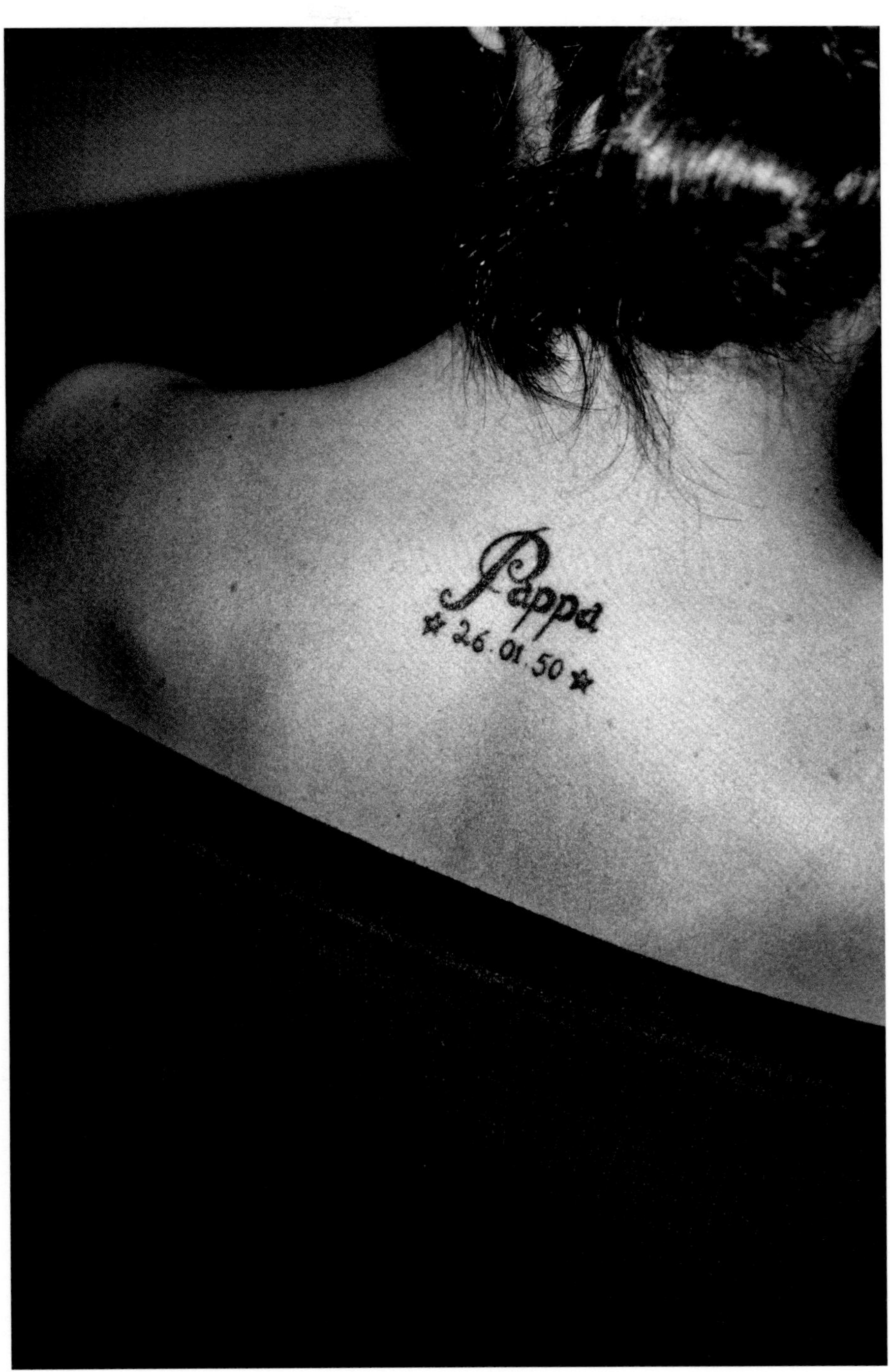
Pappa
26. 01. 50

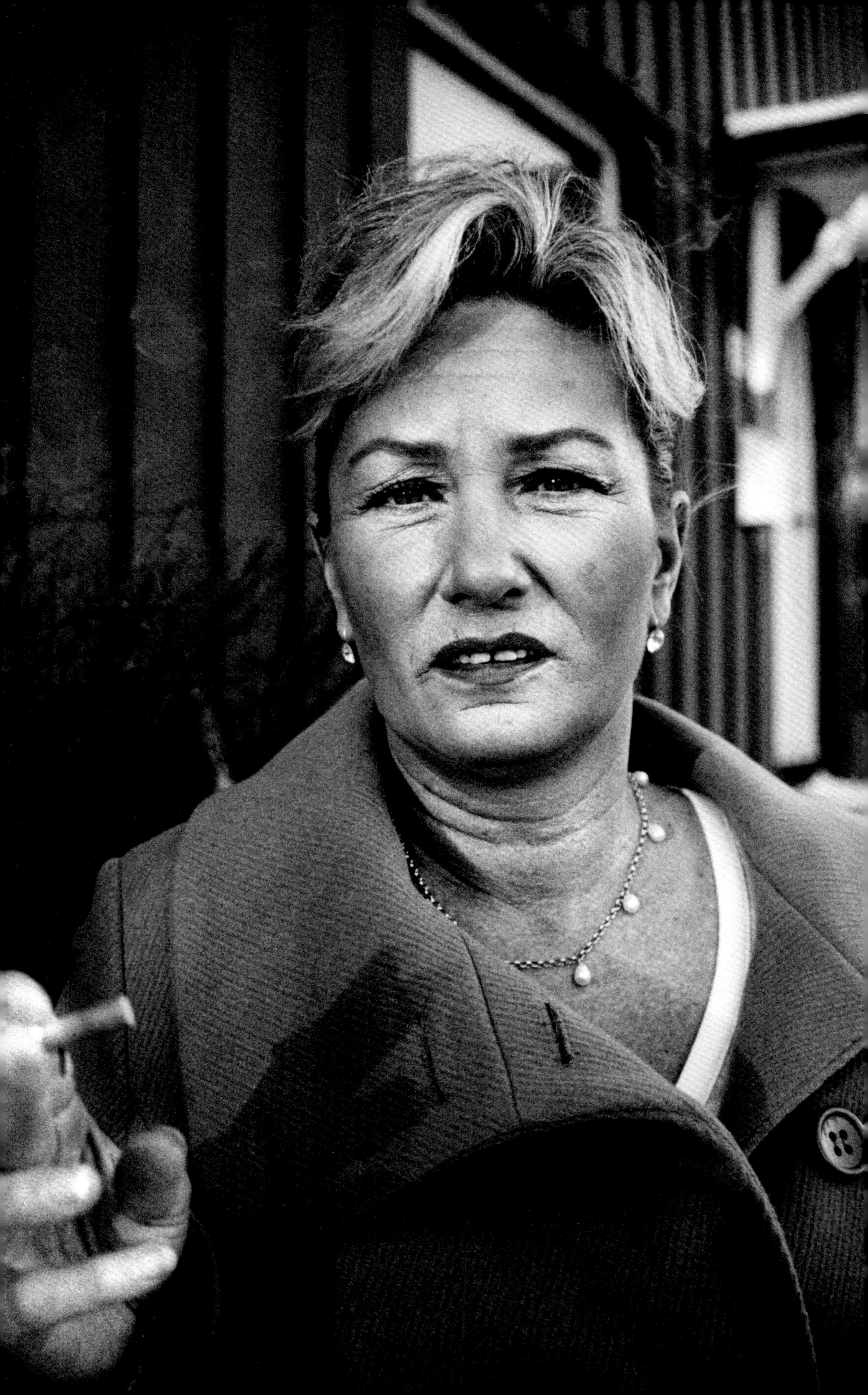

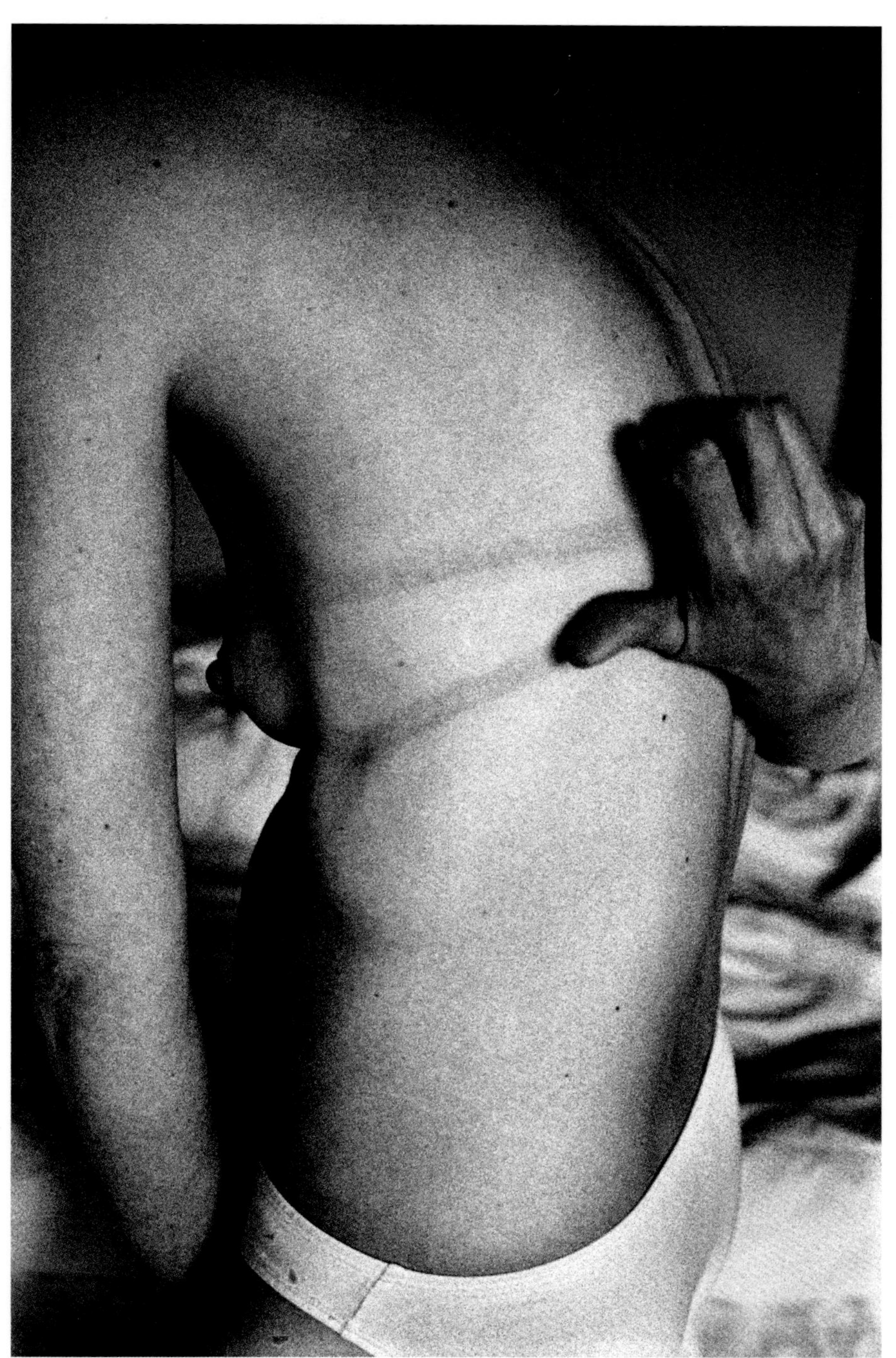

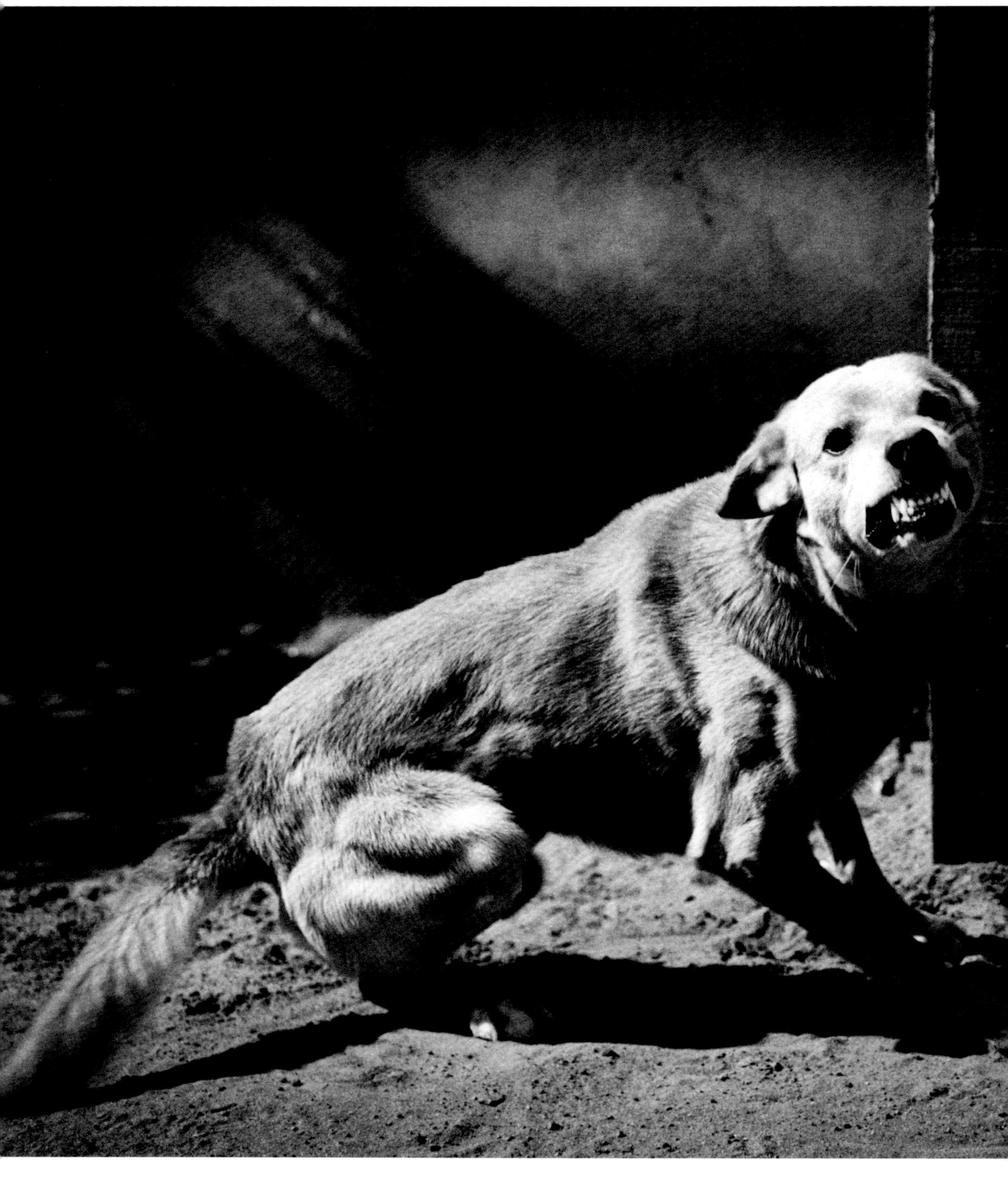

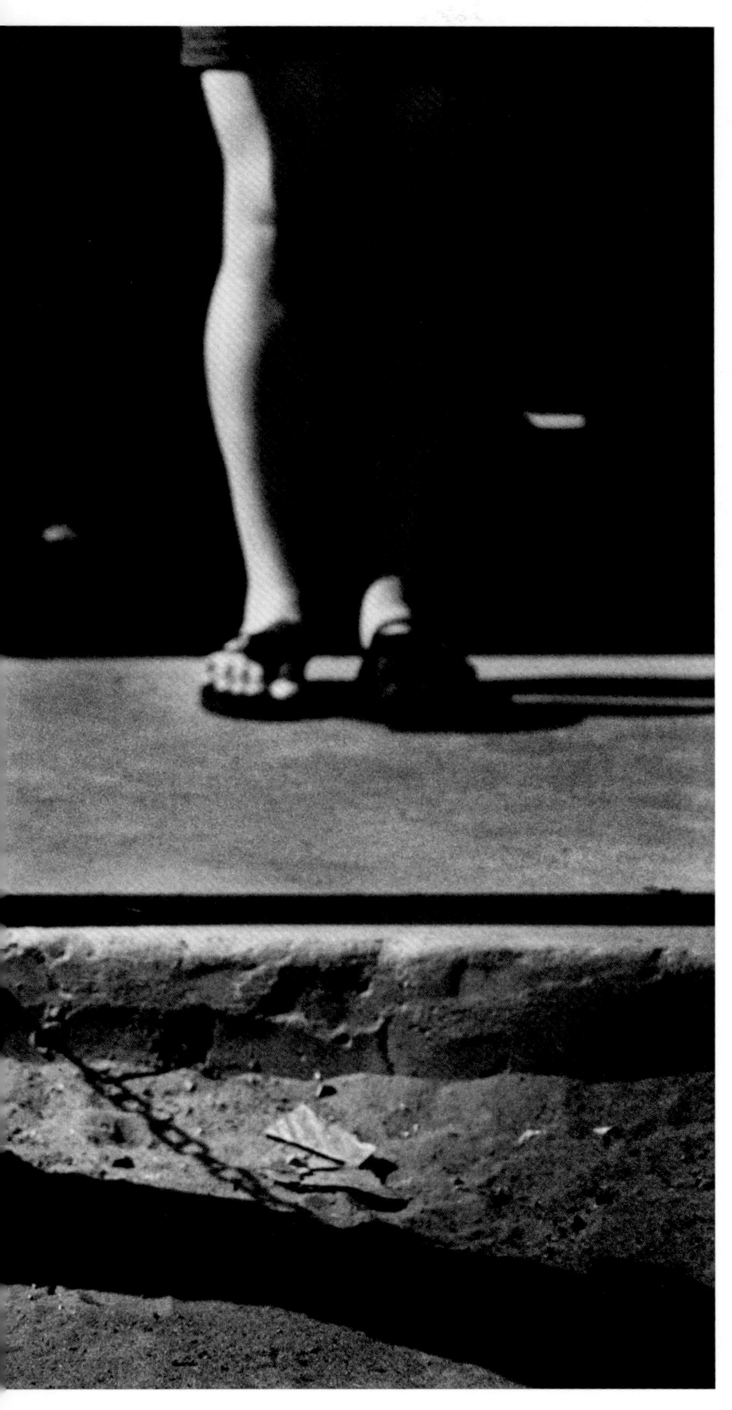

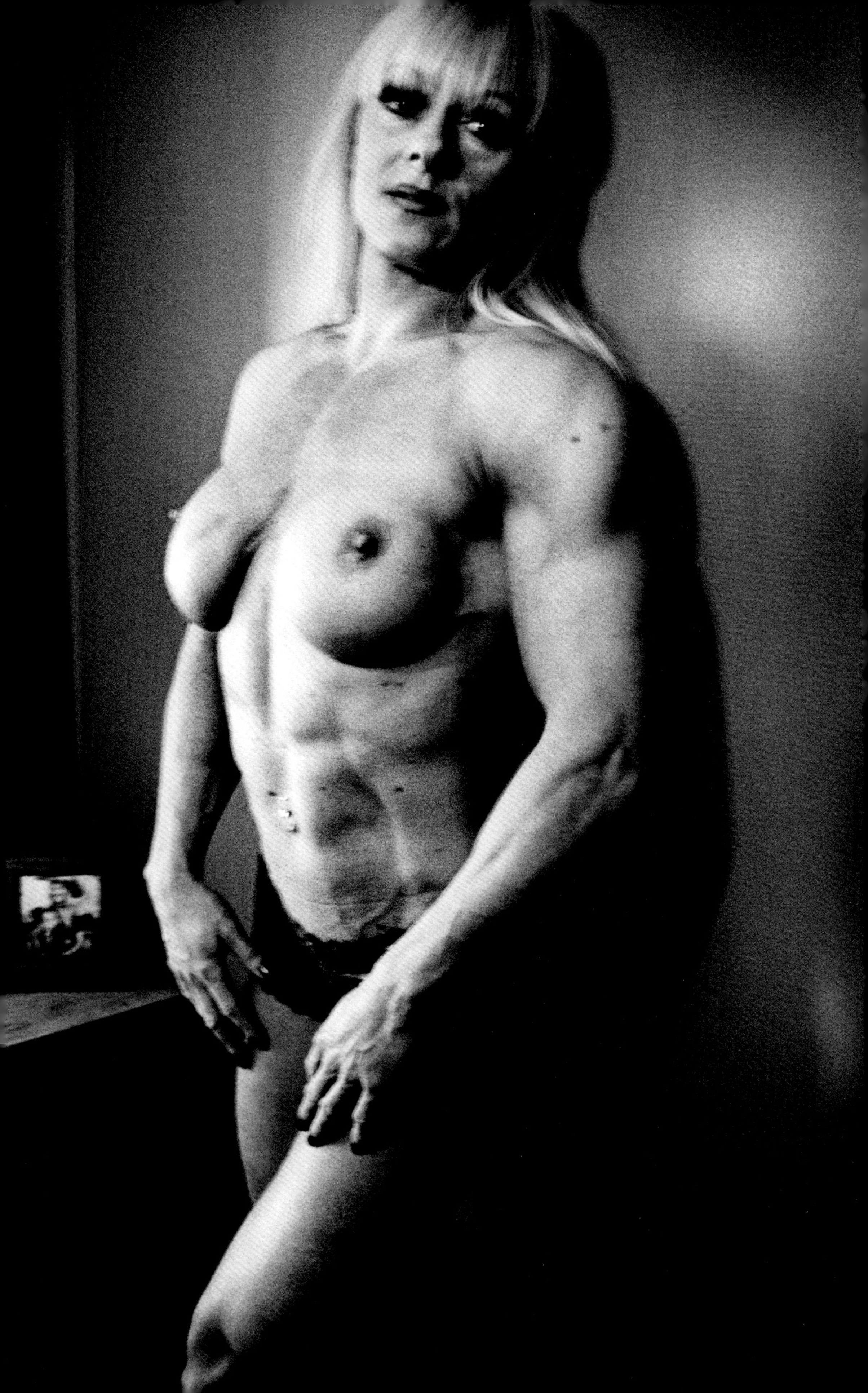

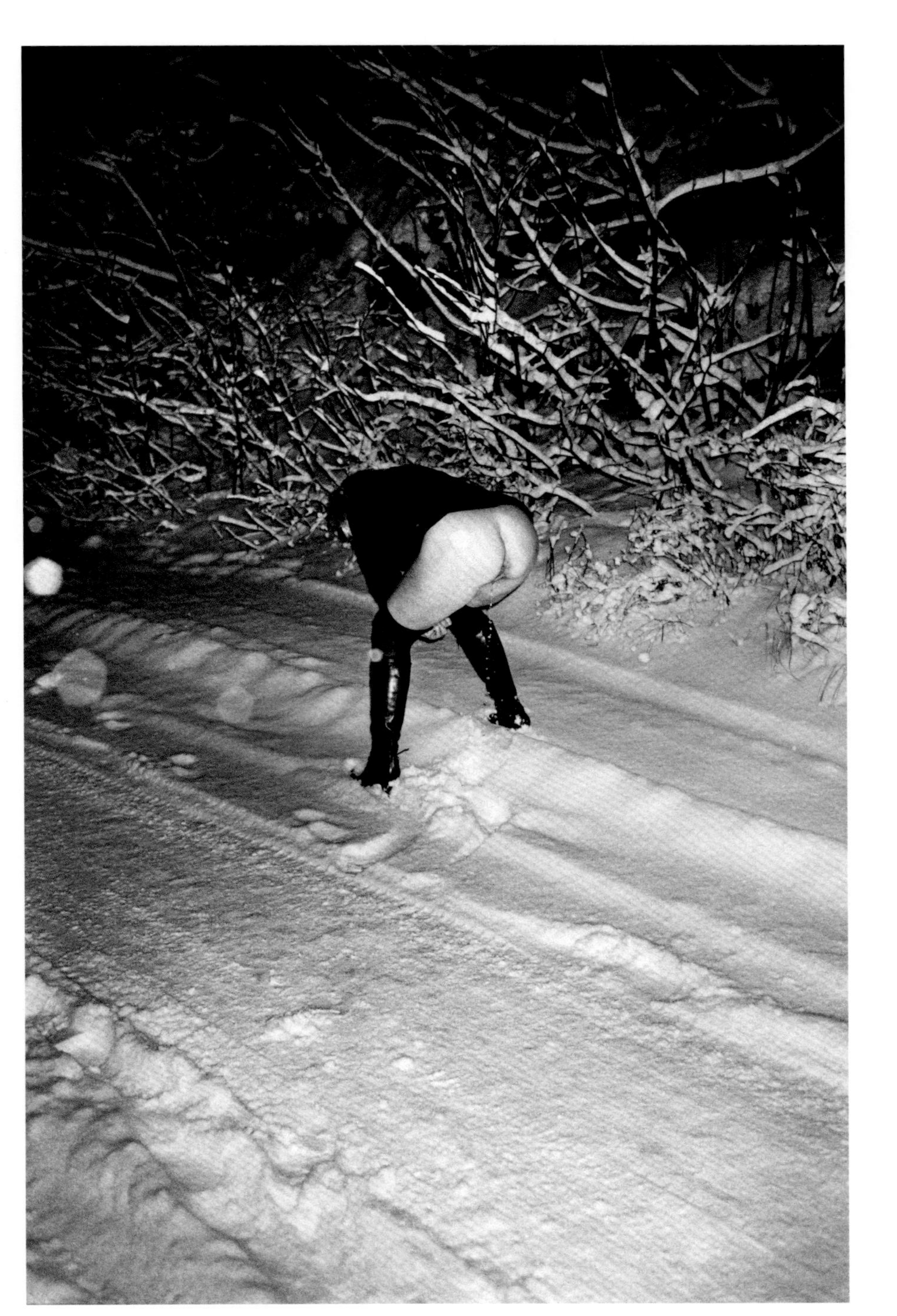

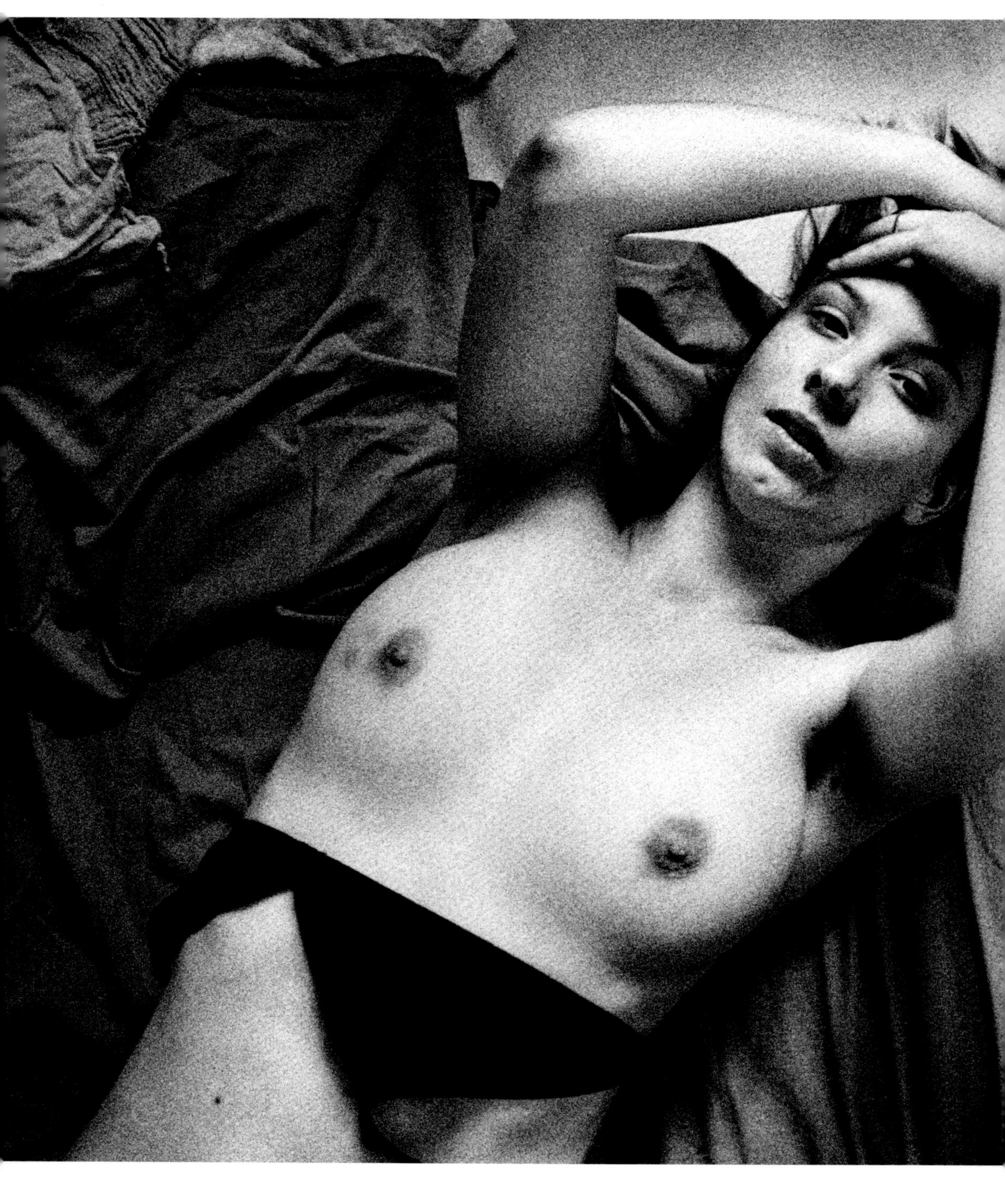

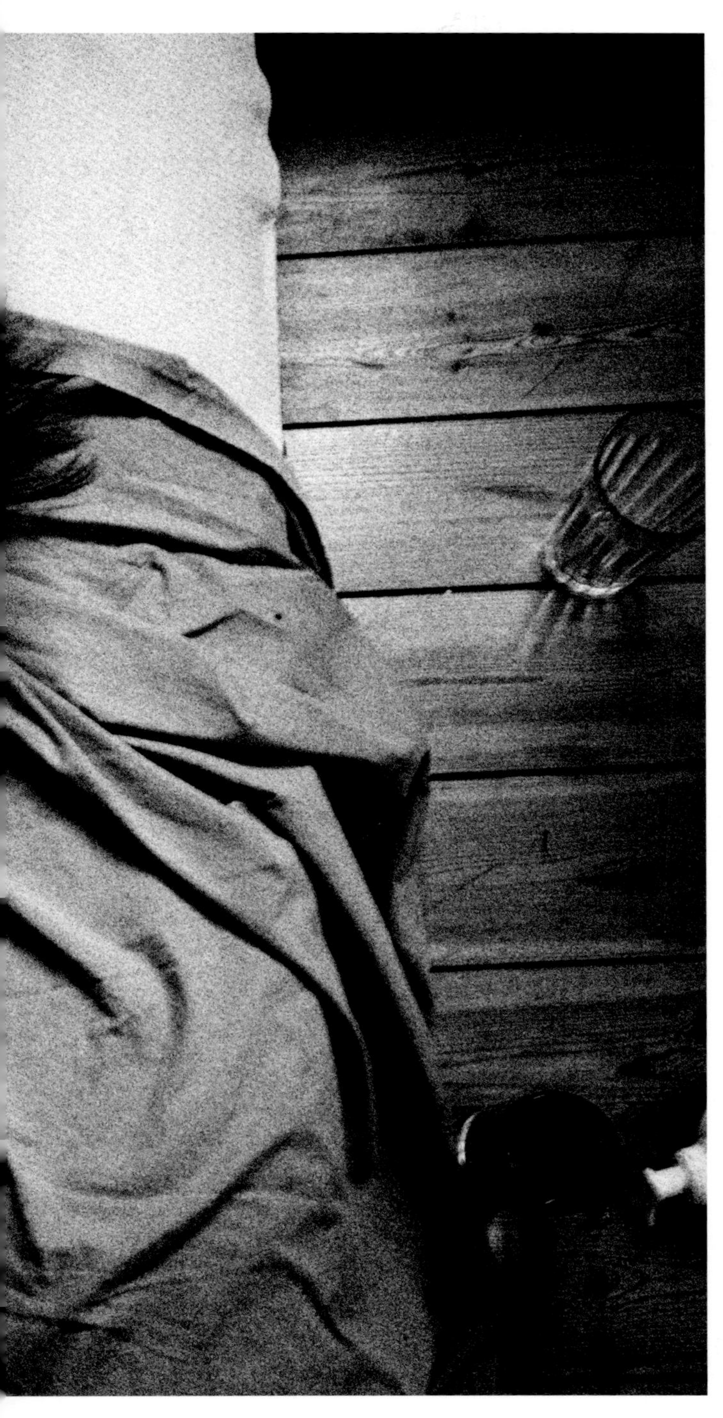

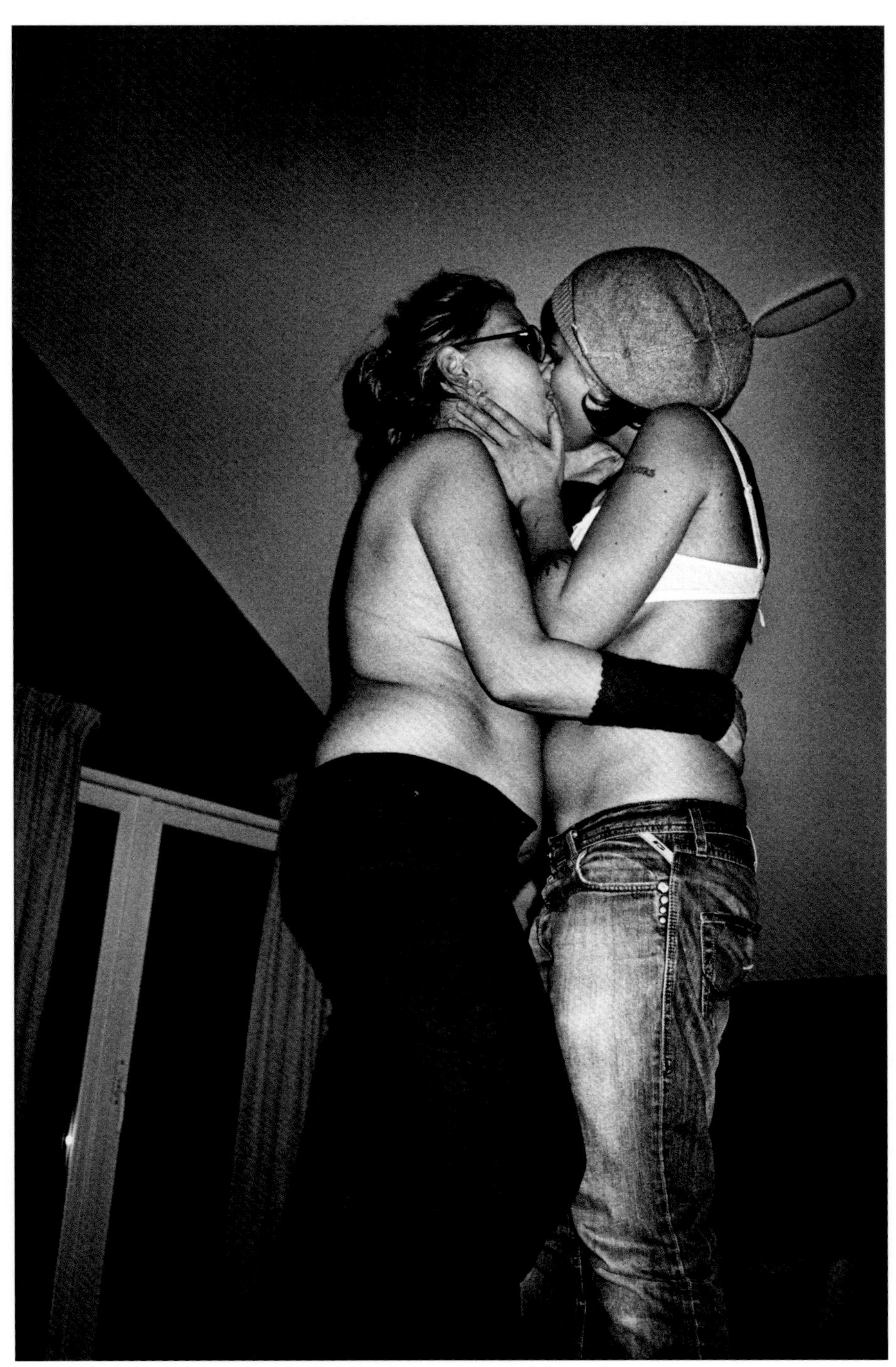

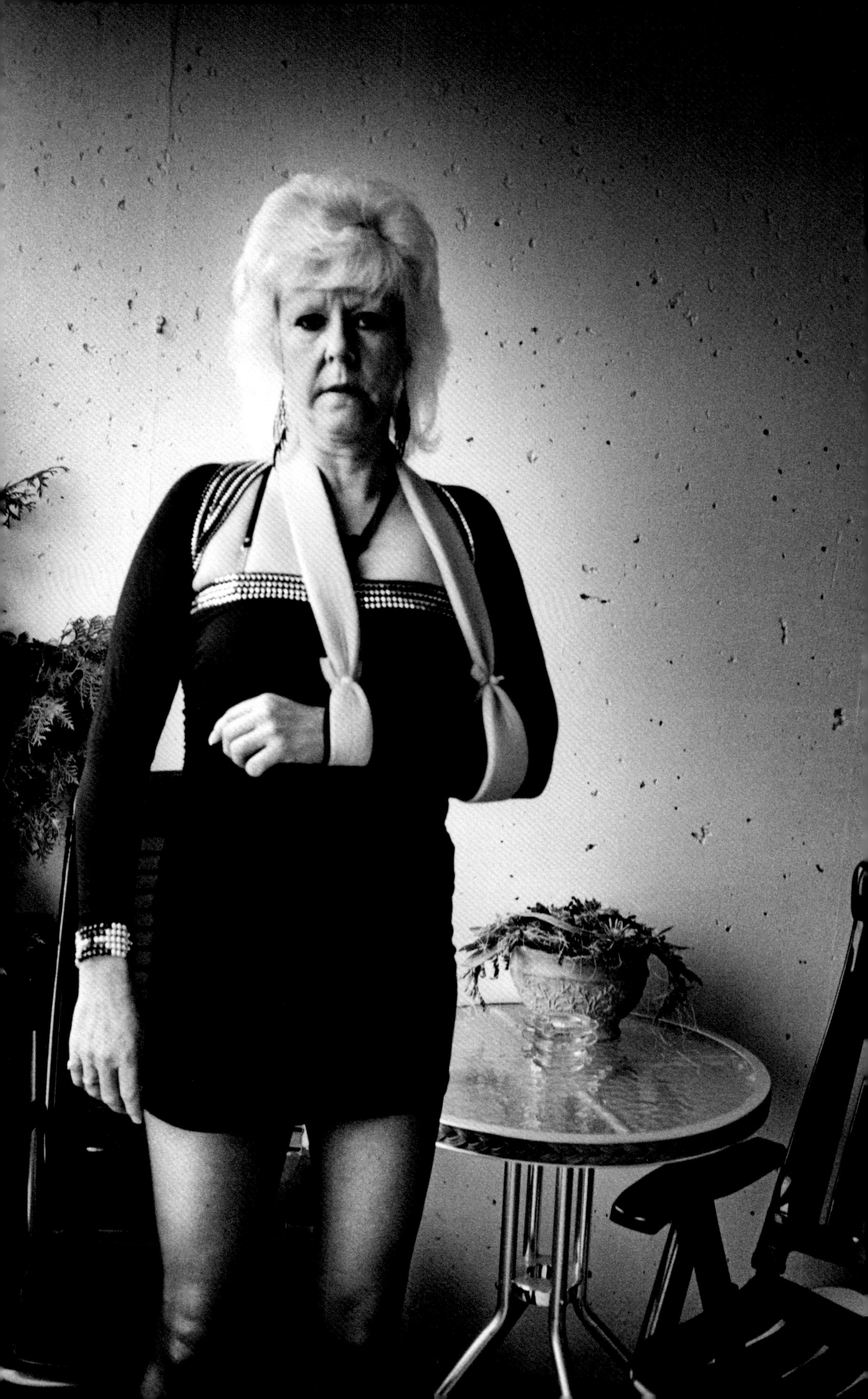

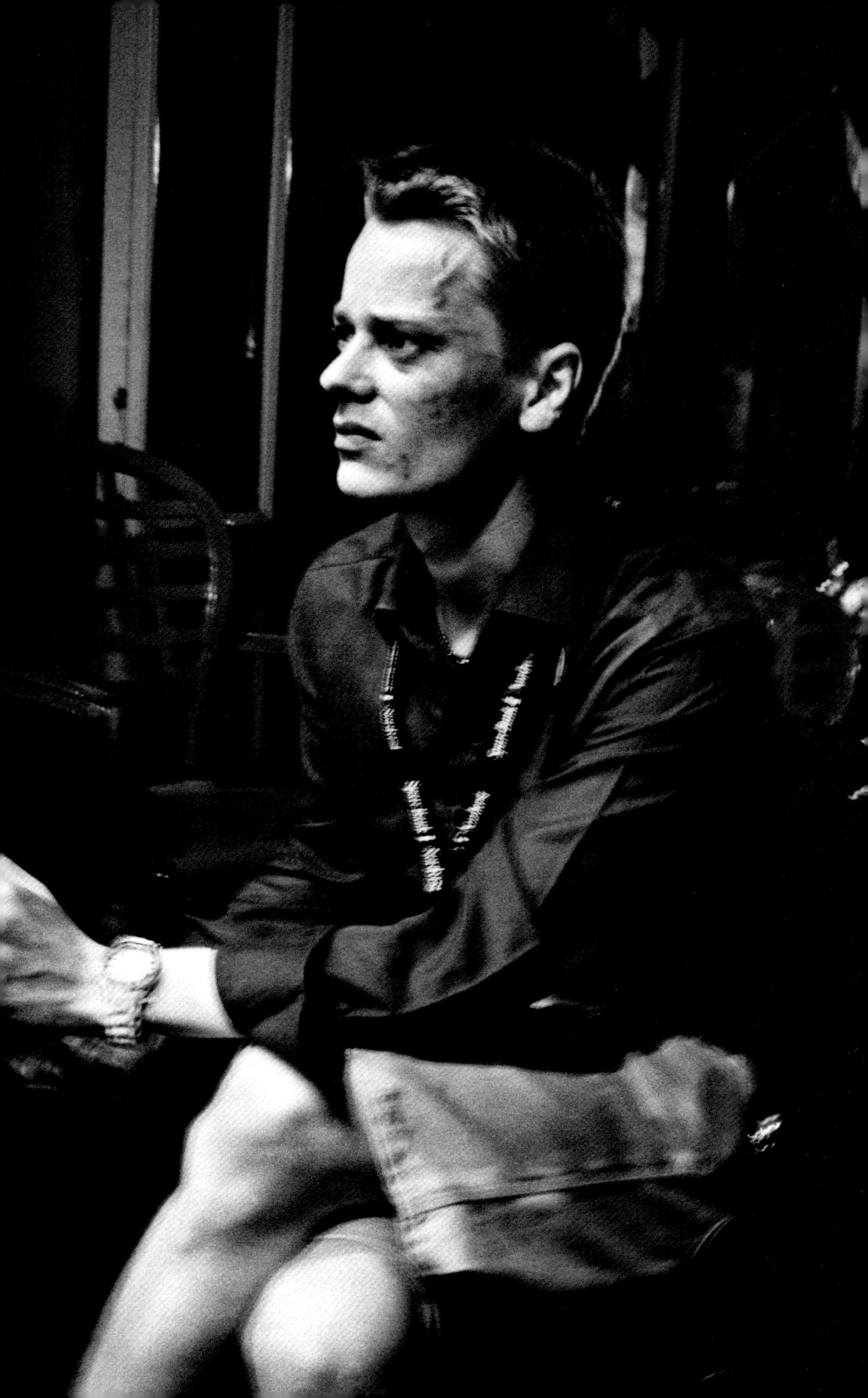

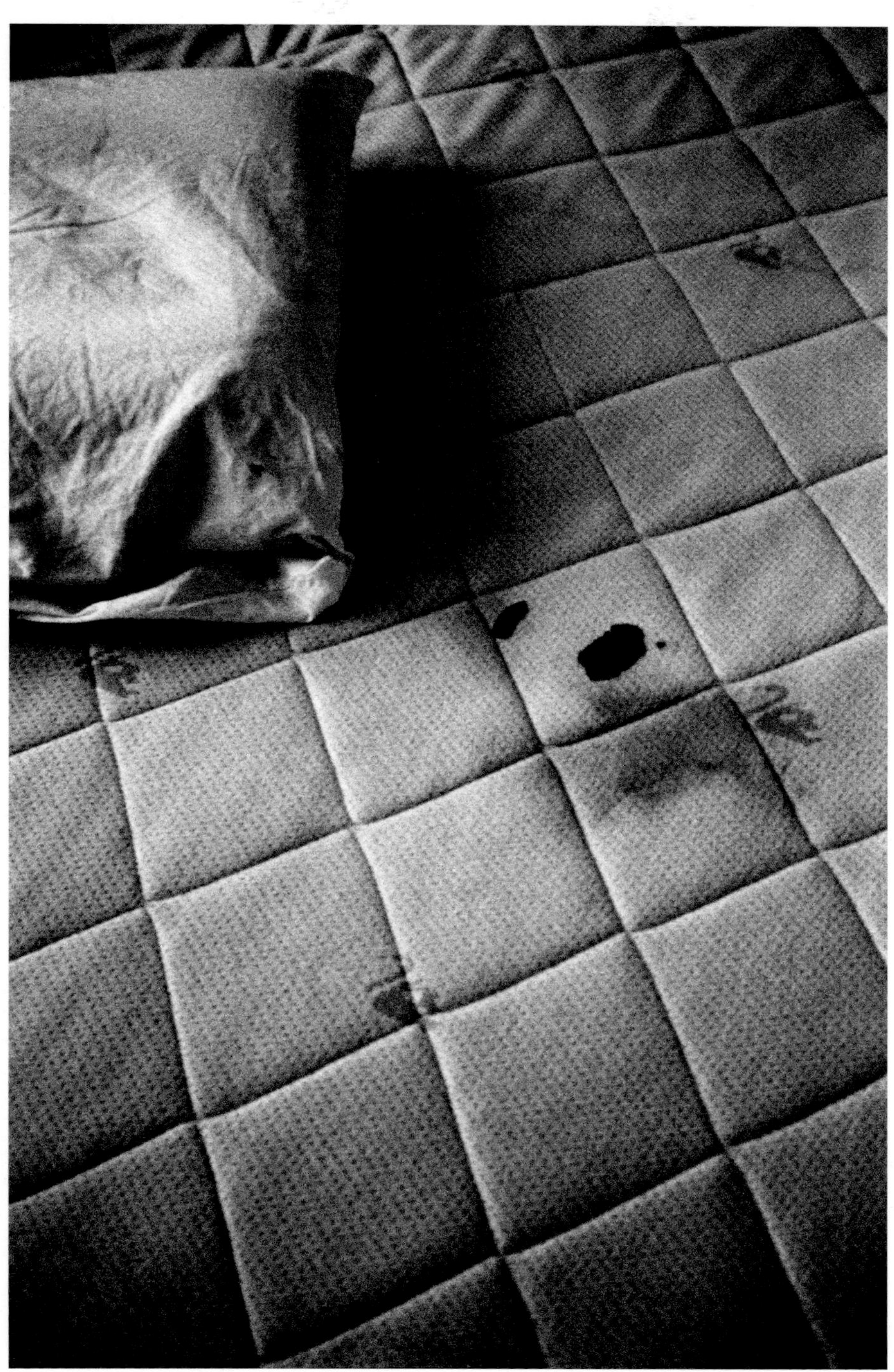

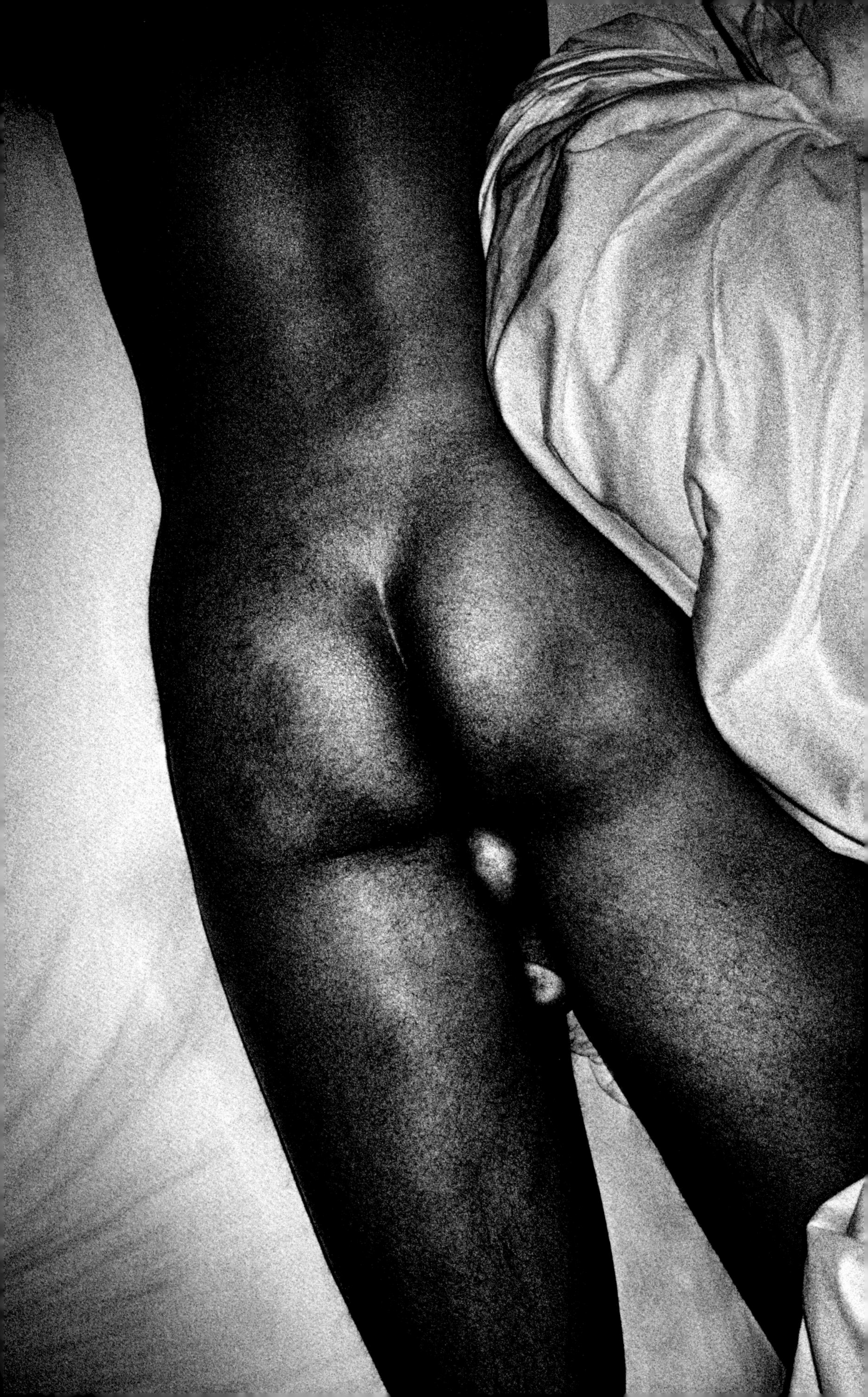

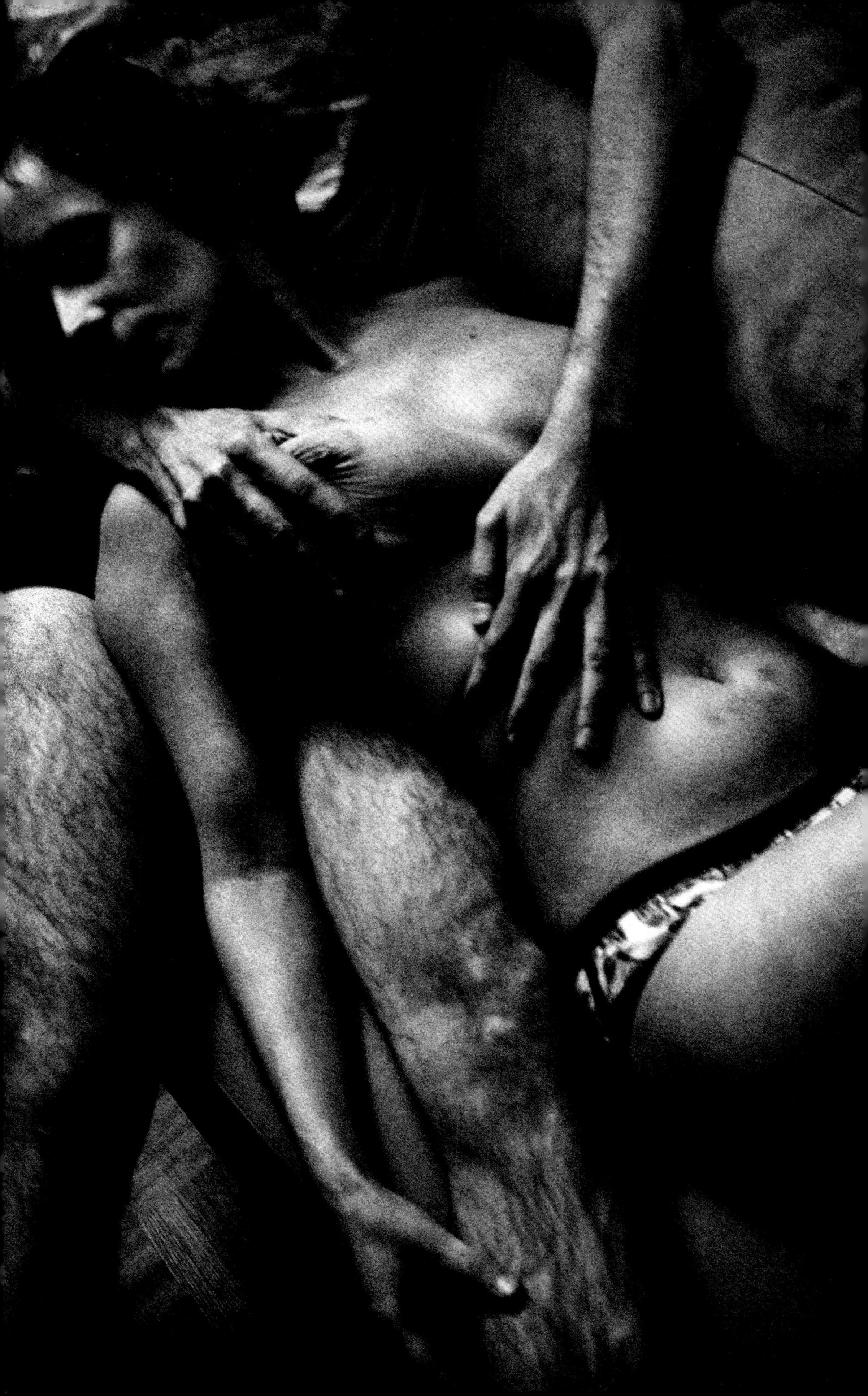

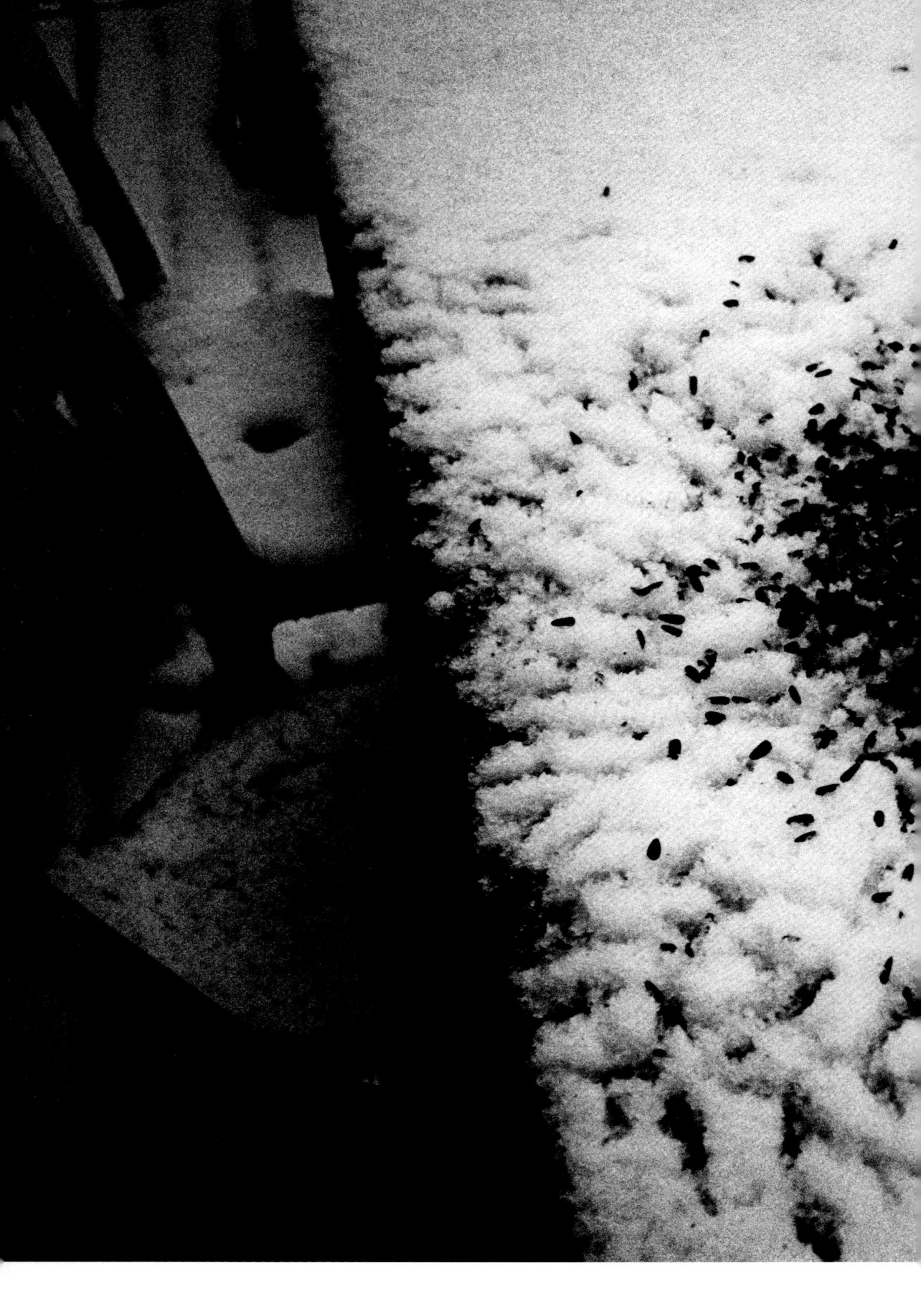

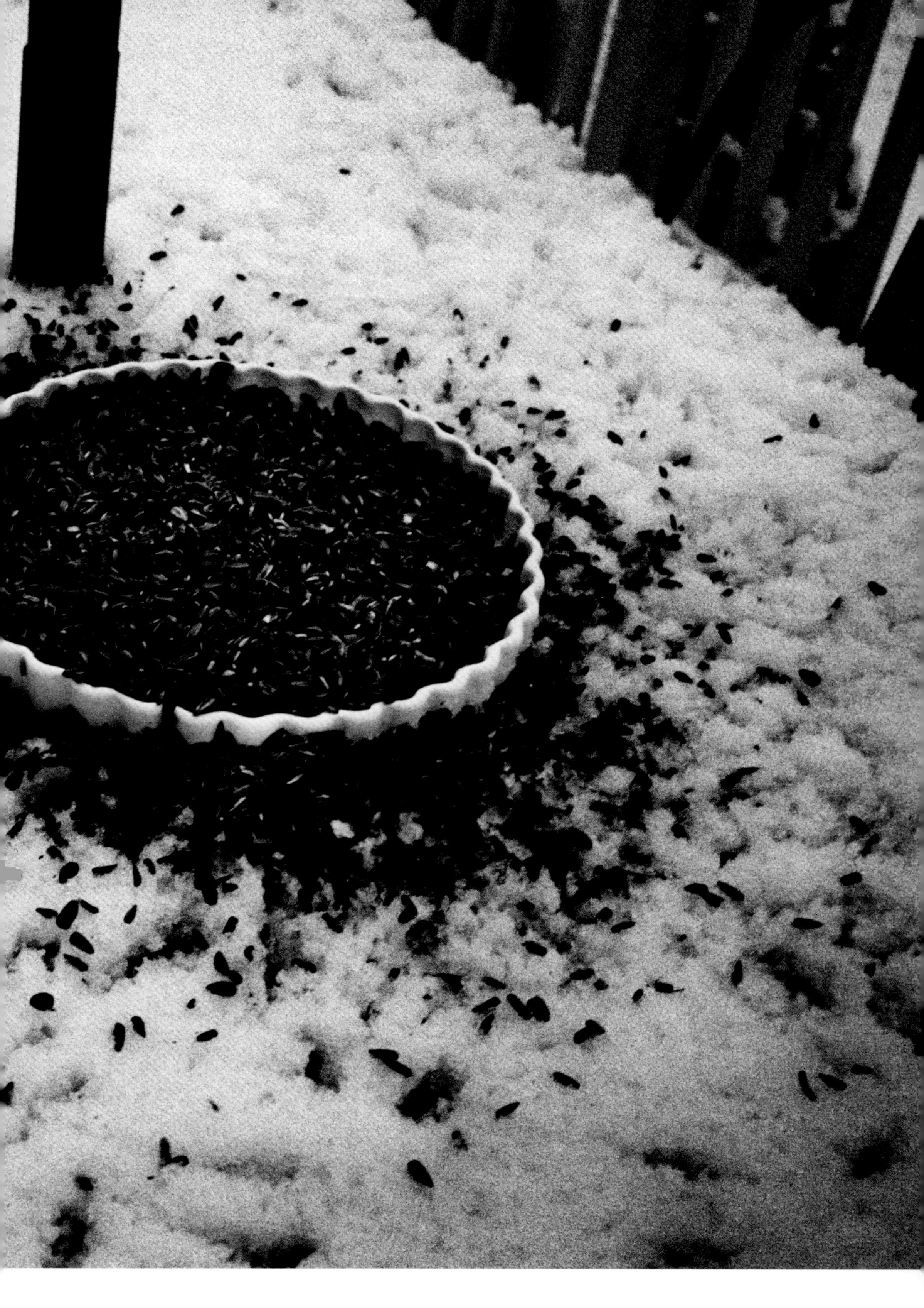

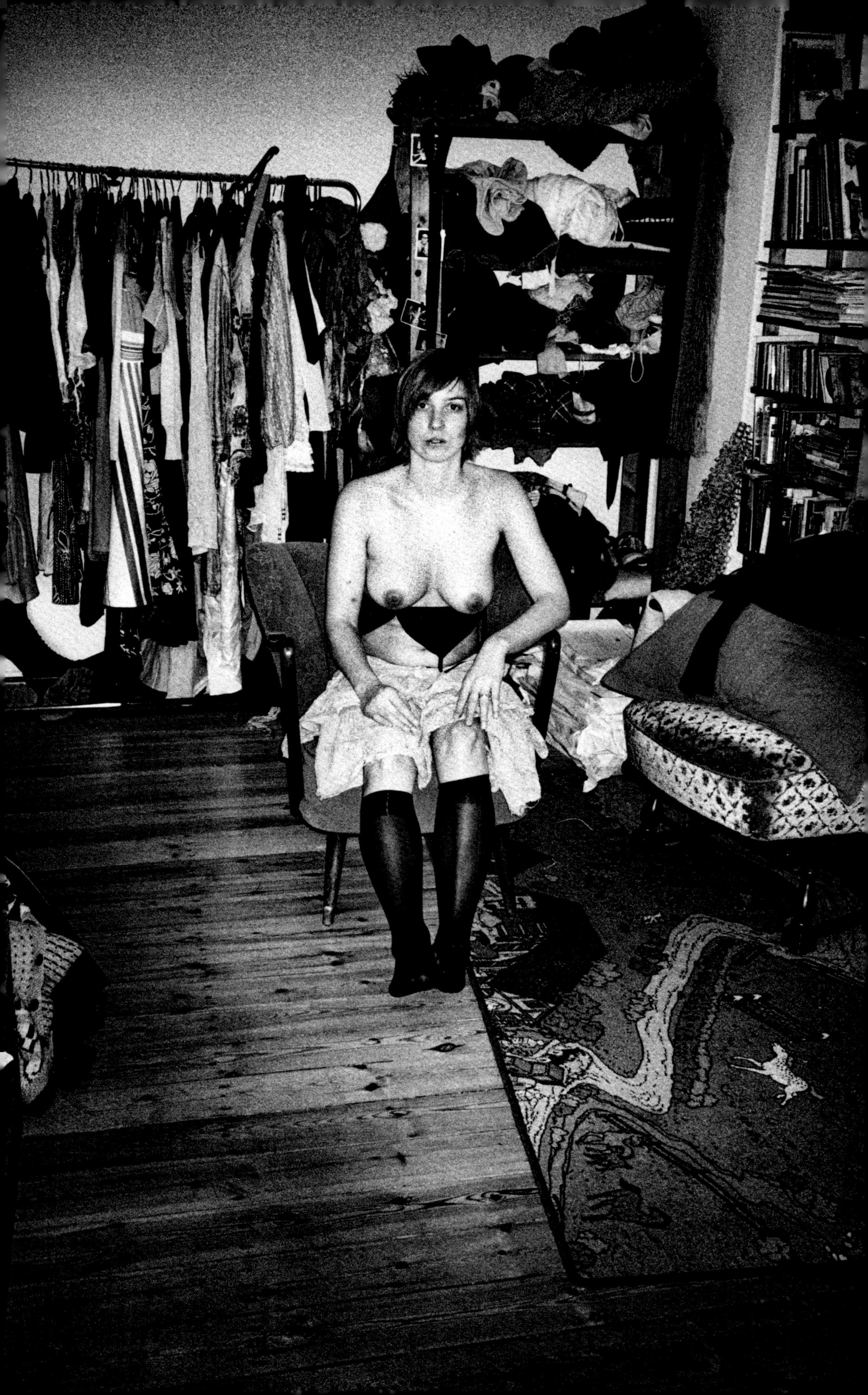

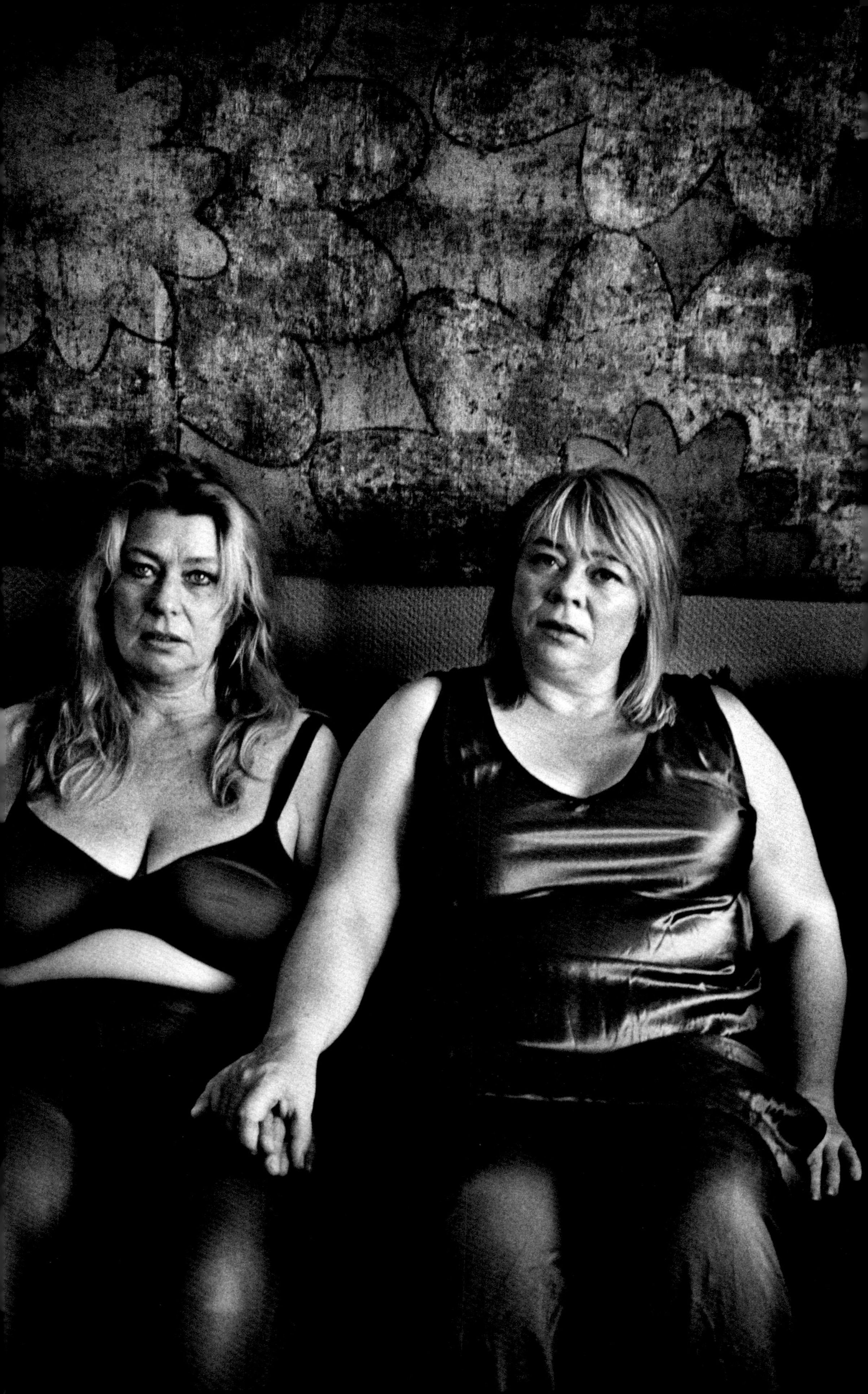

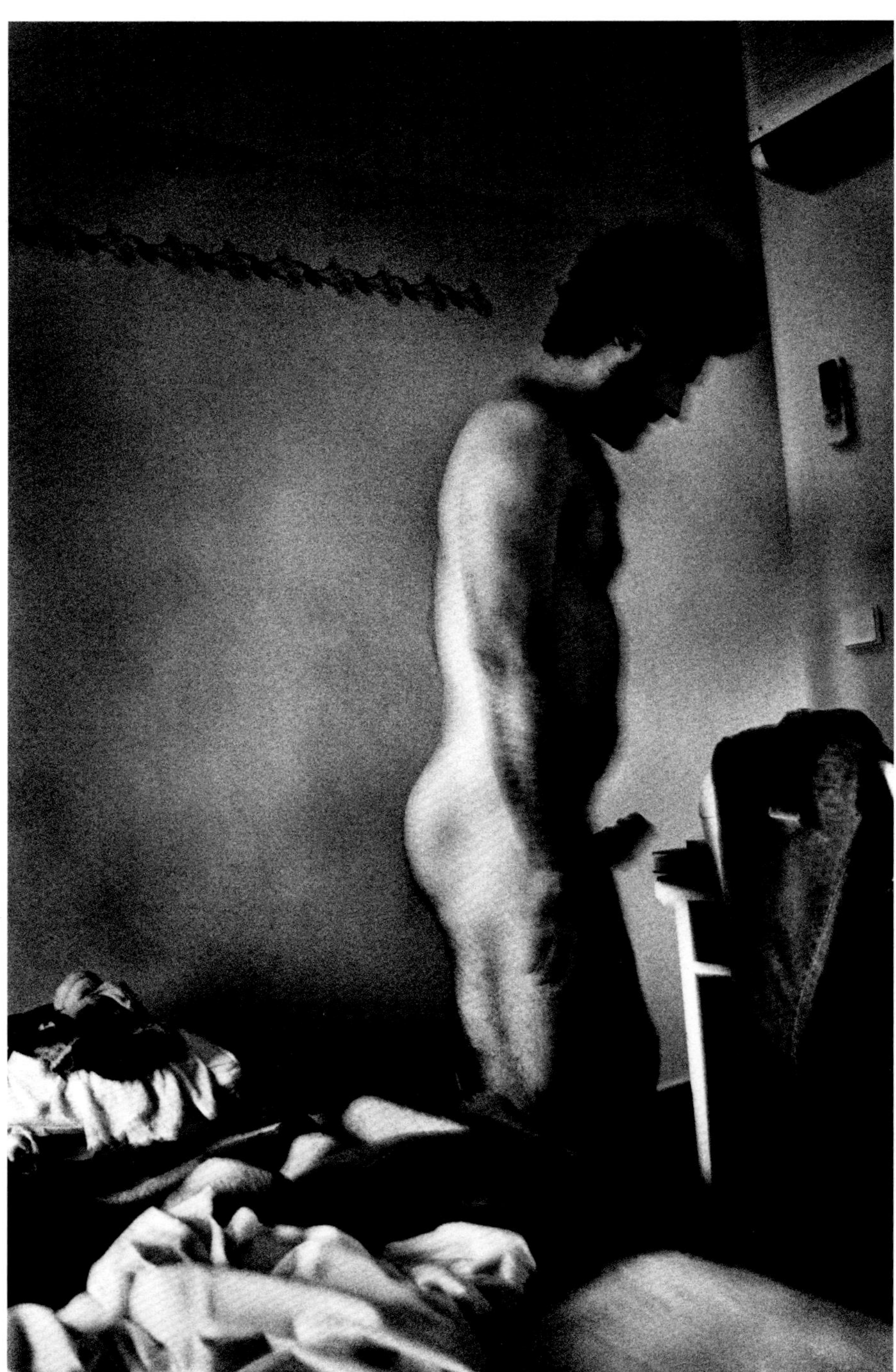

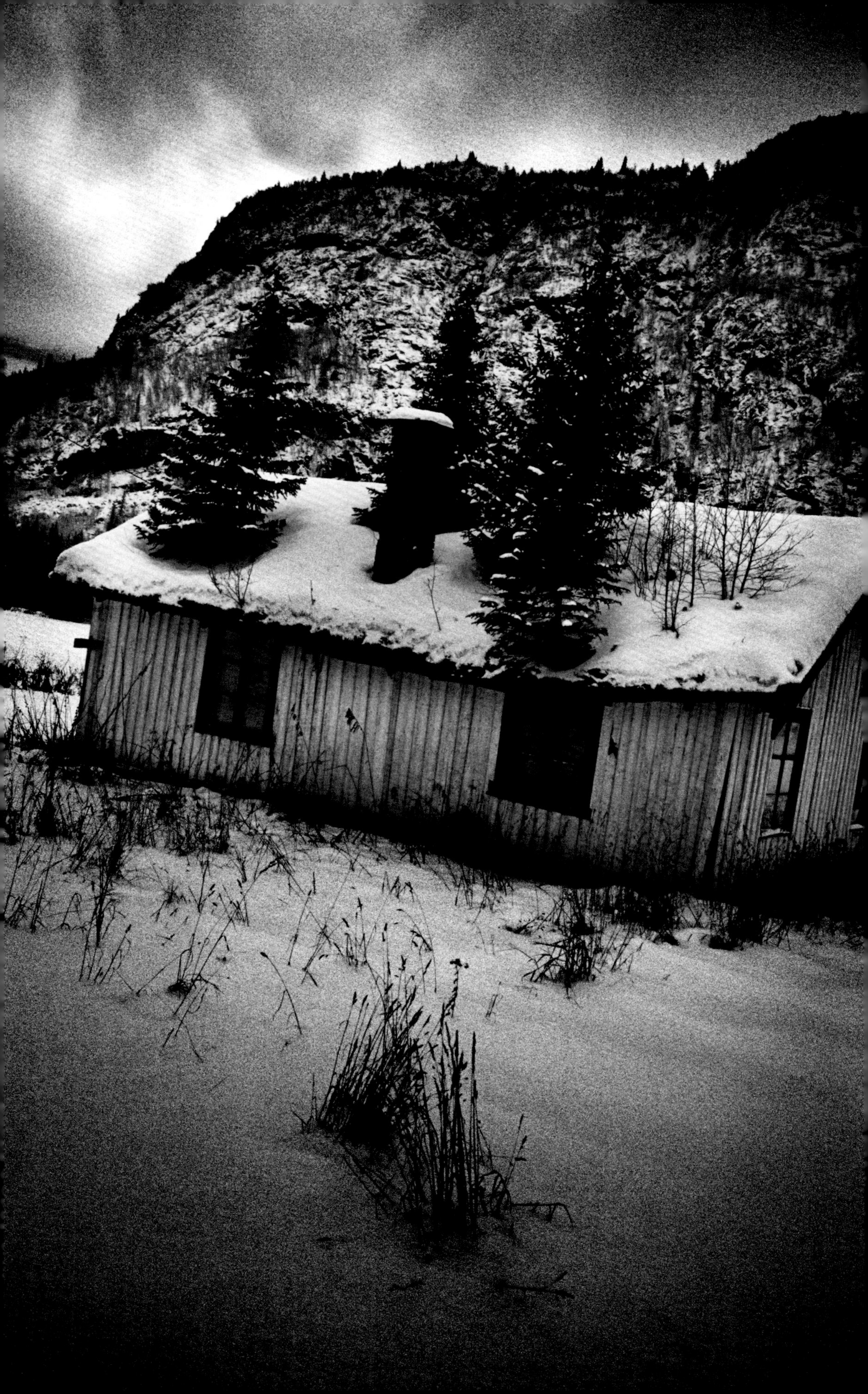

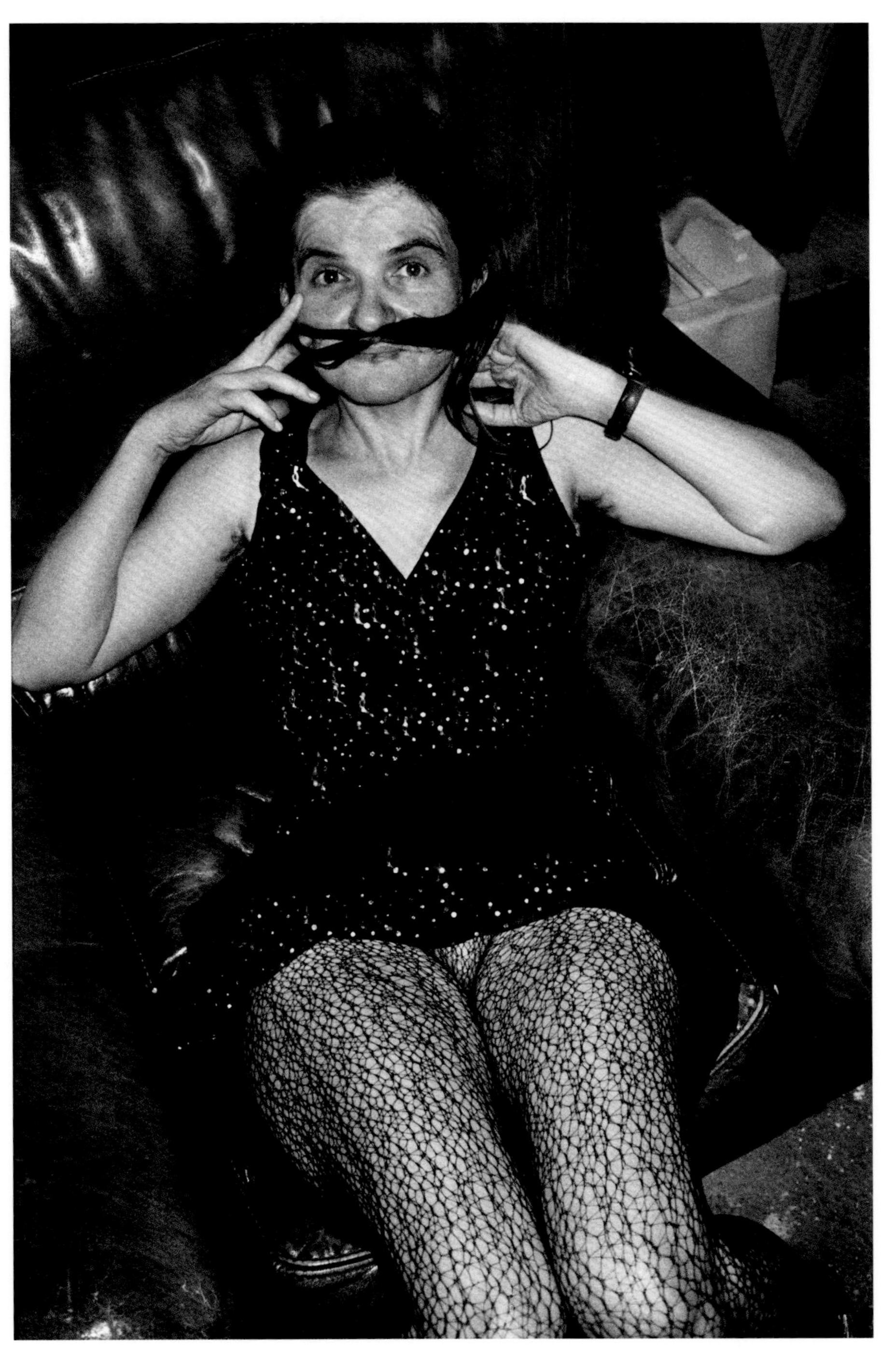

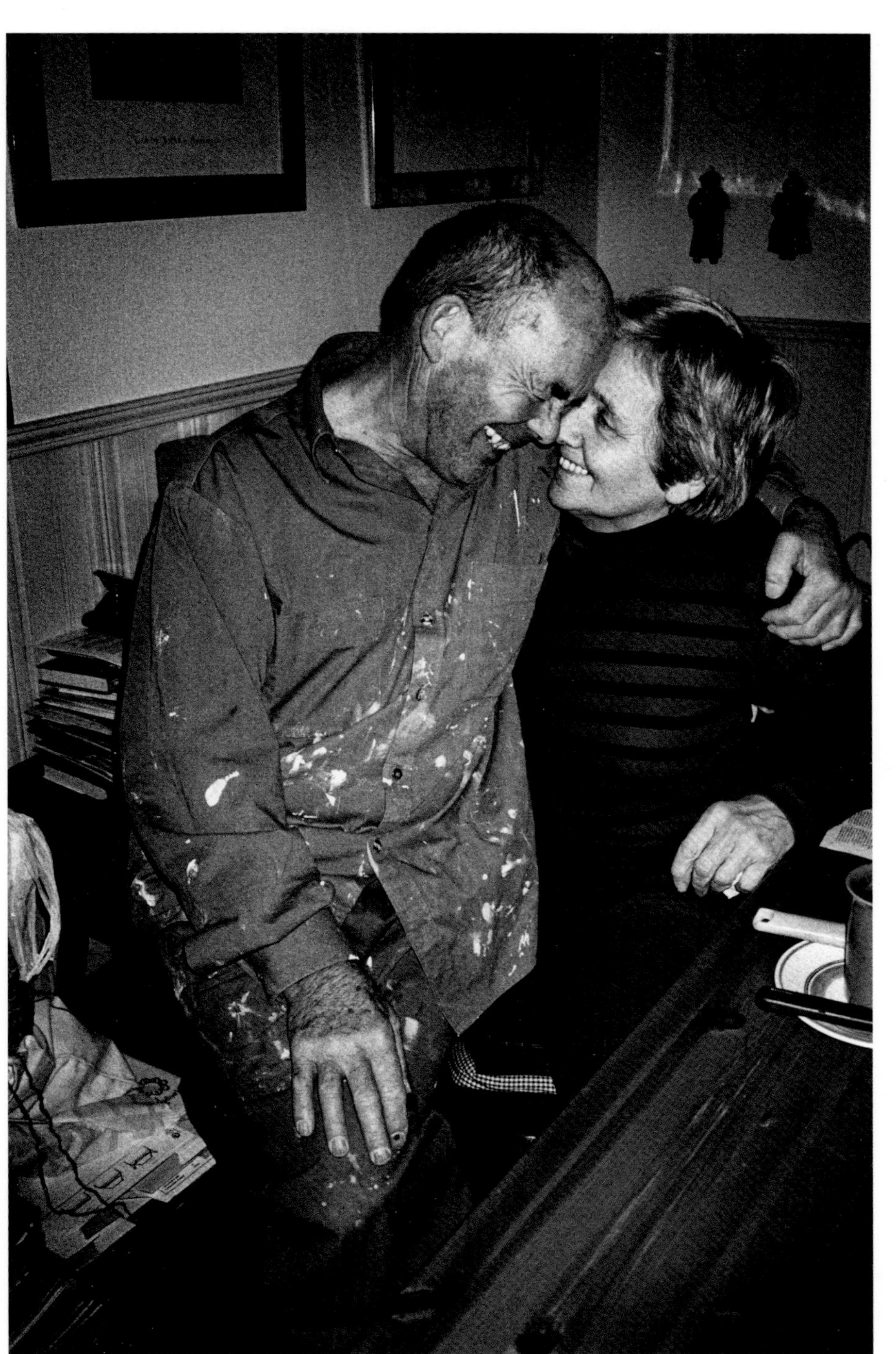

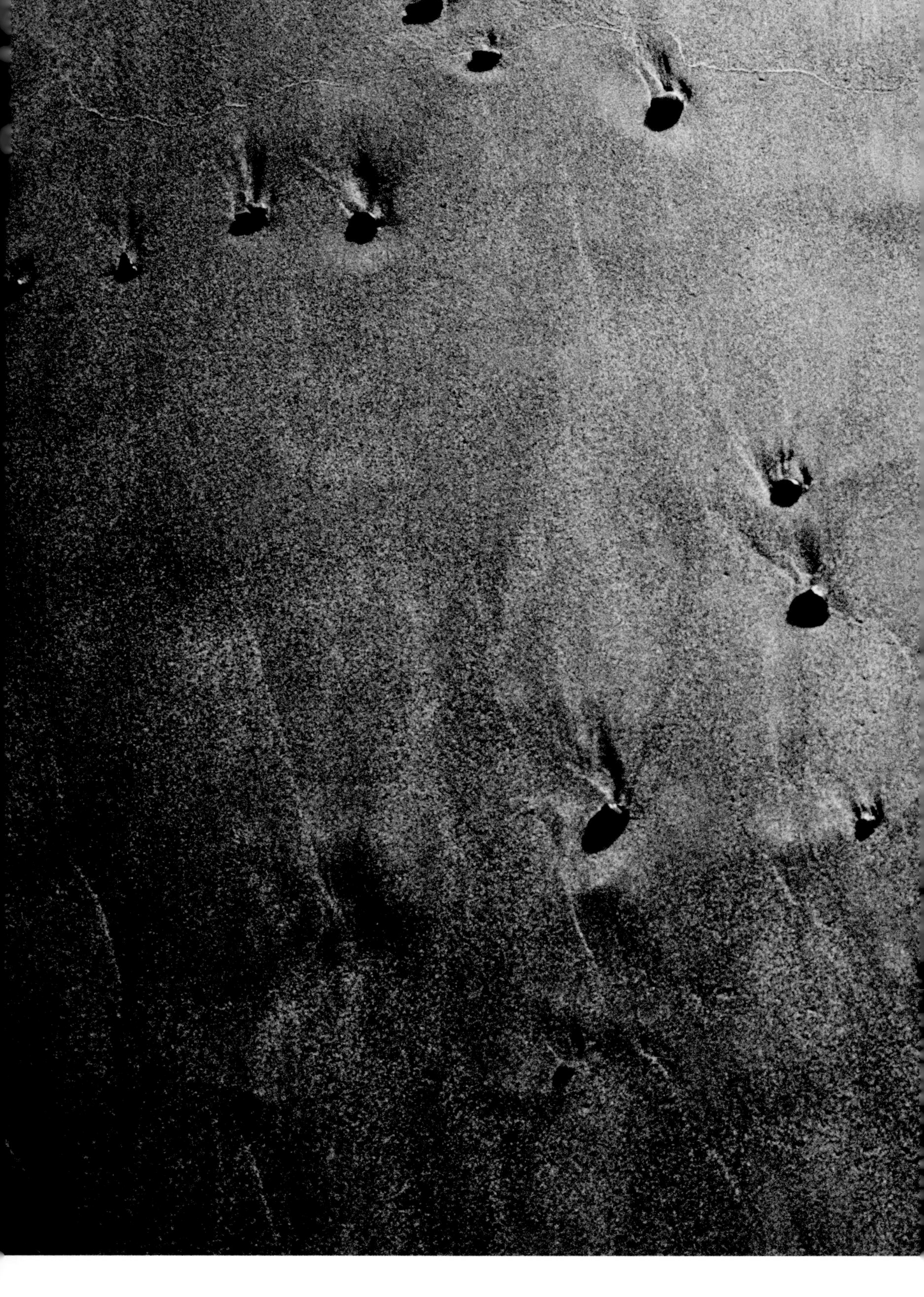

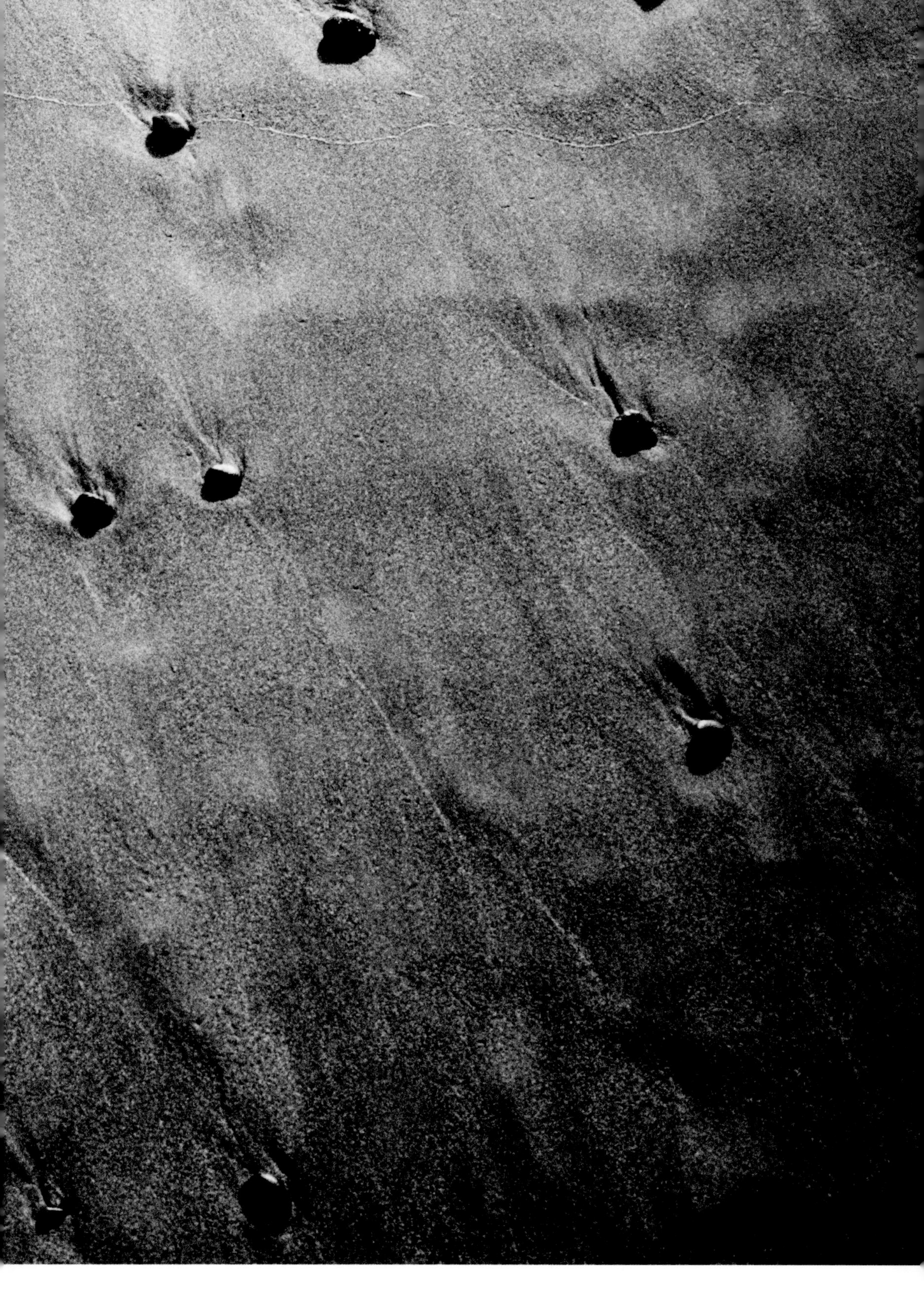

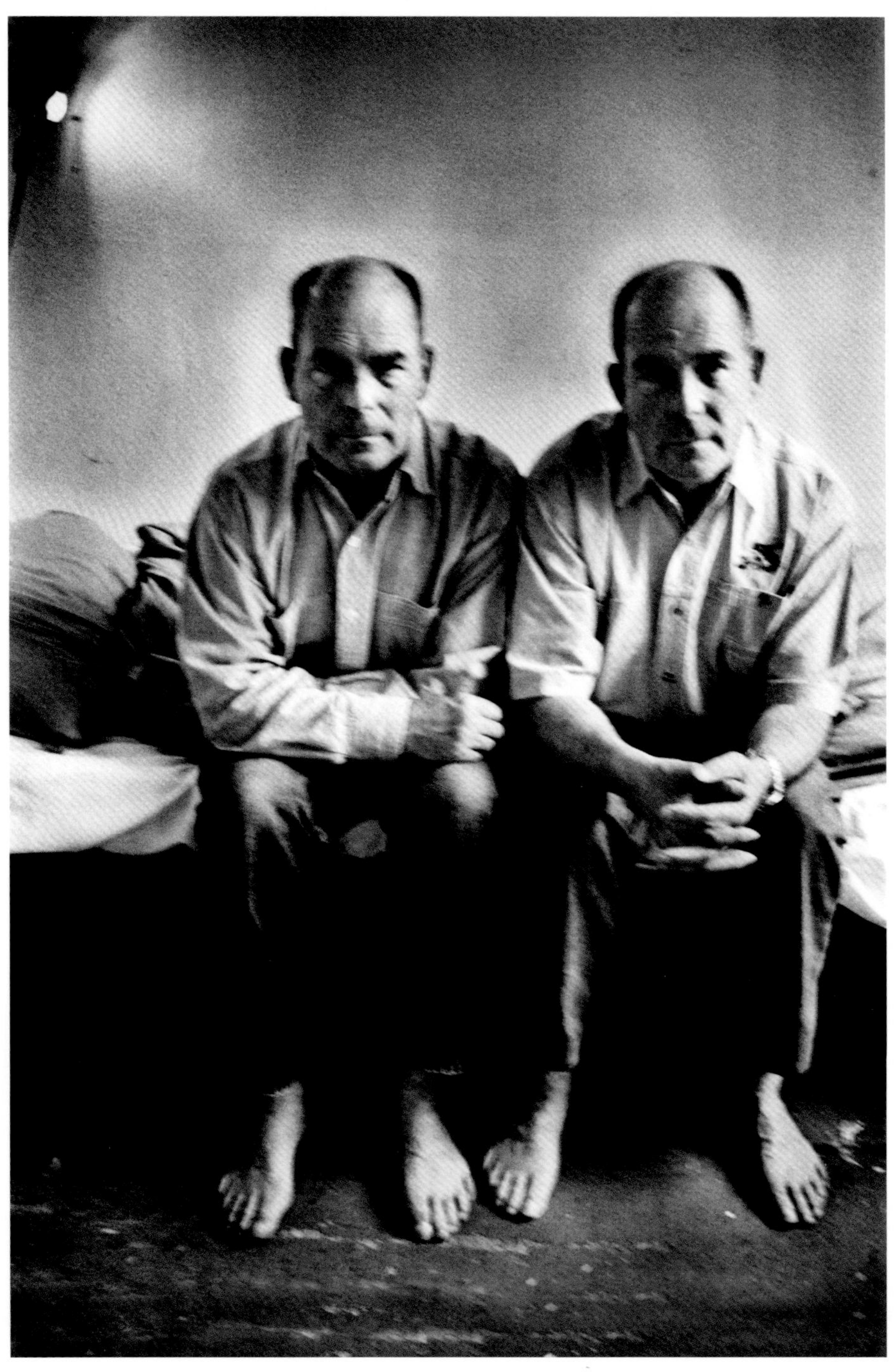

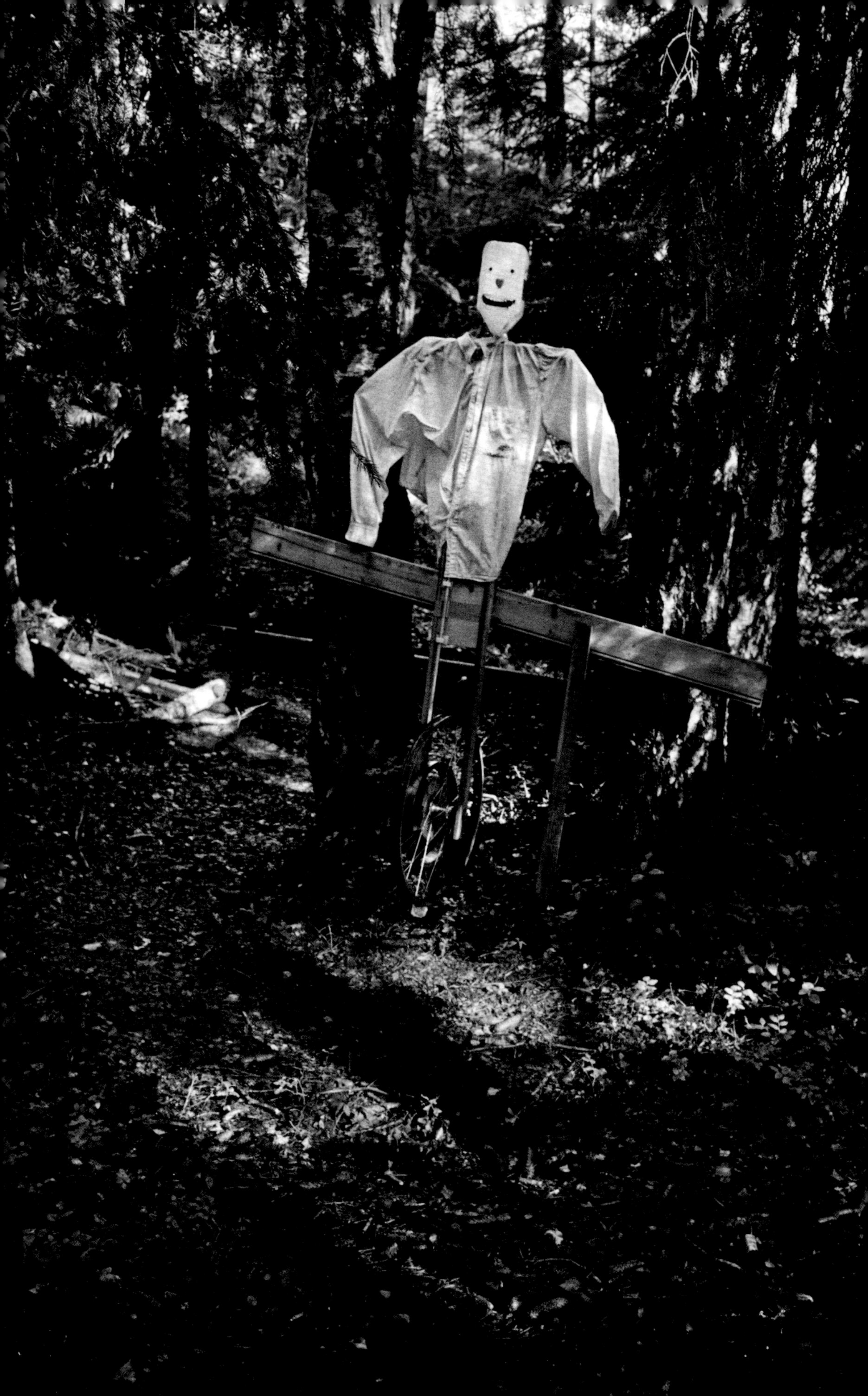

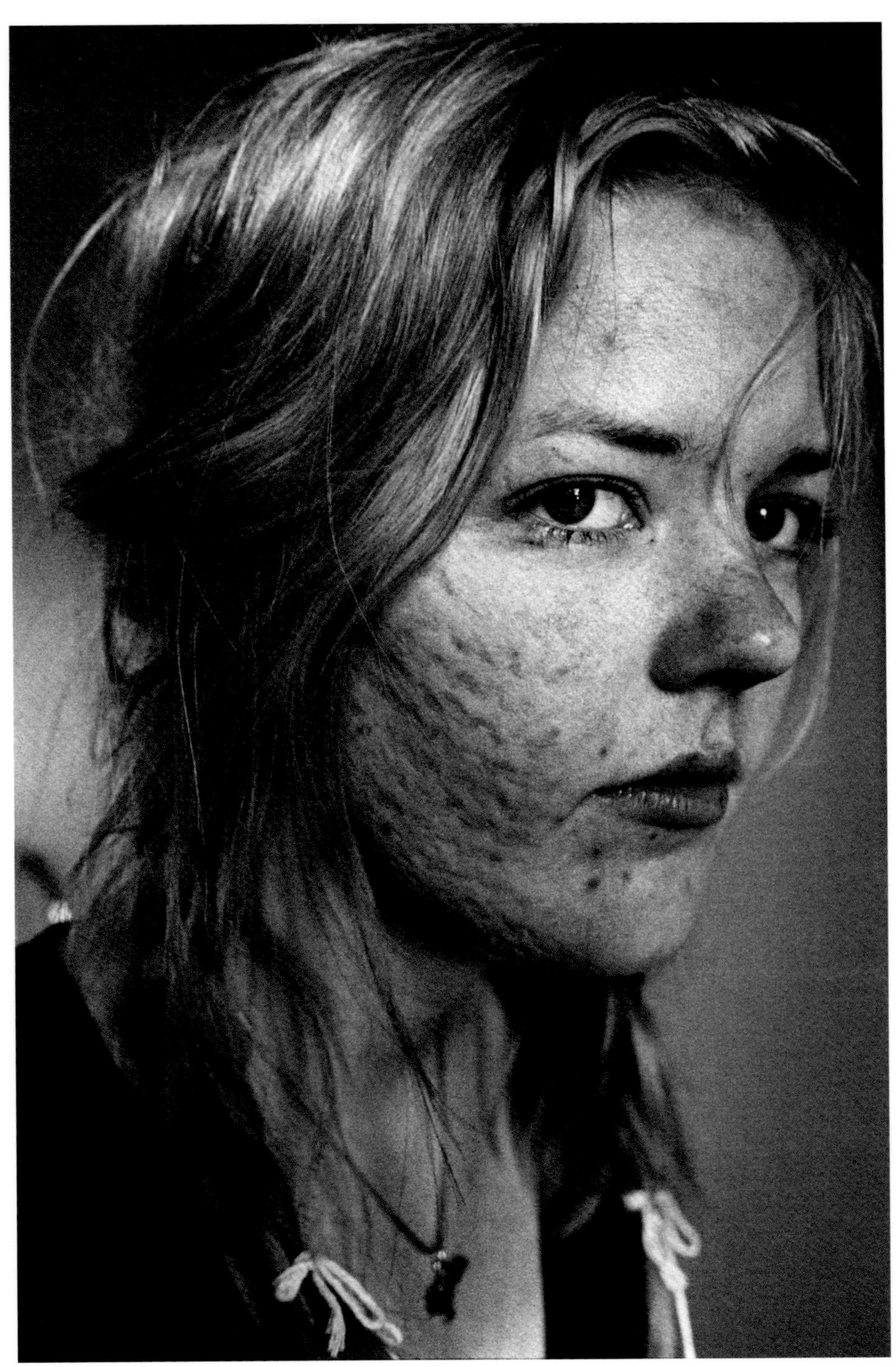

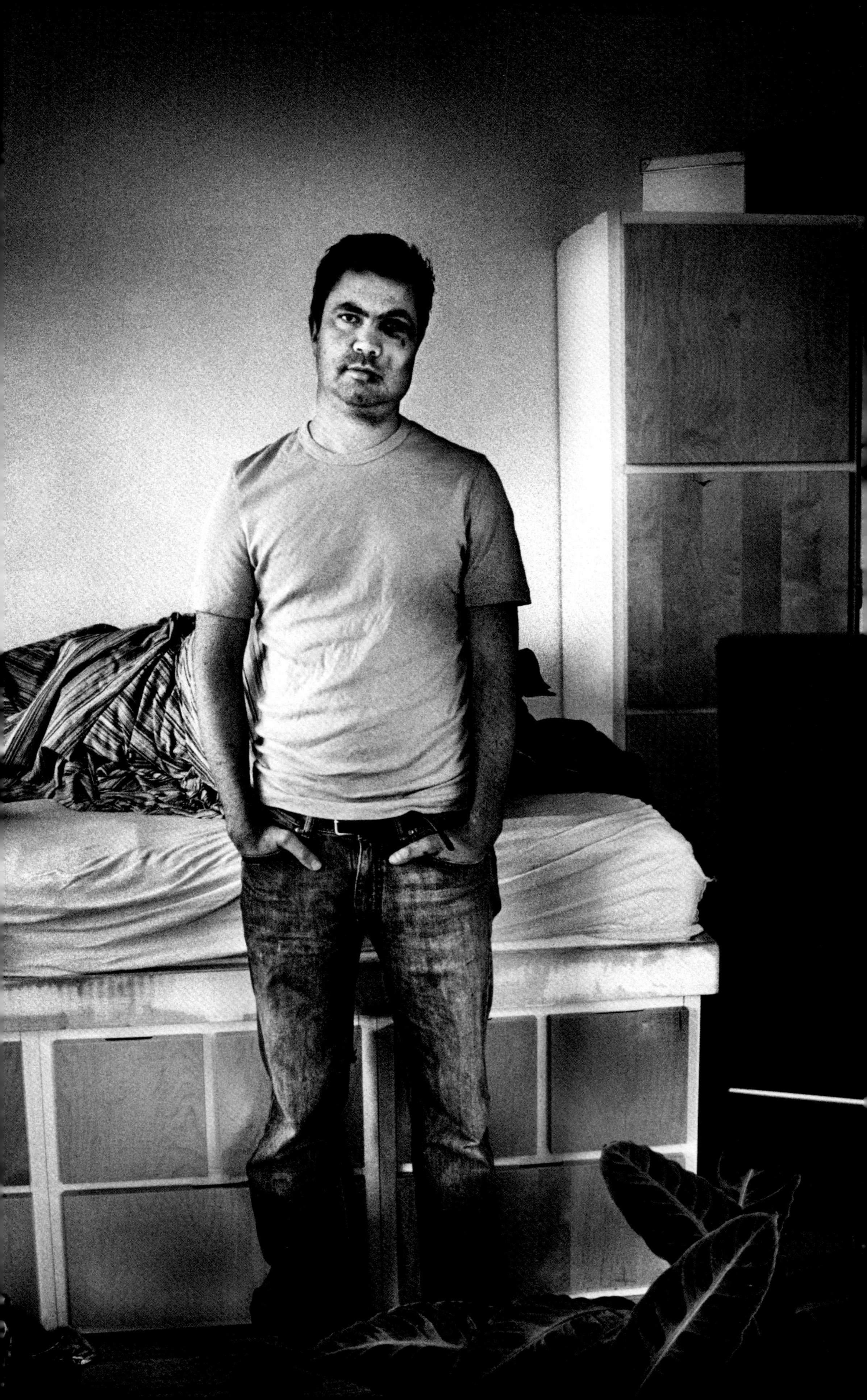

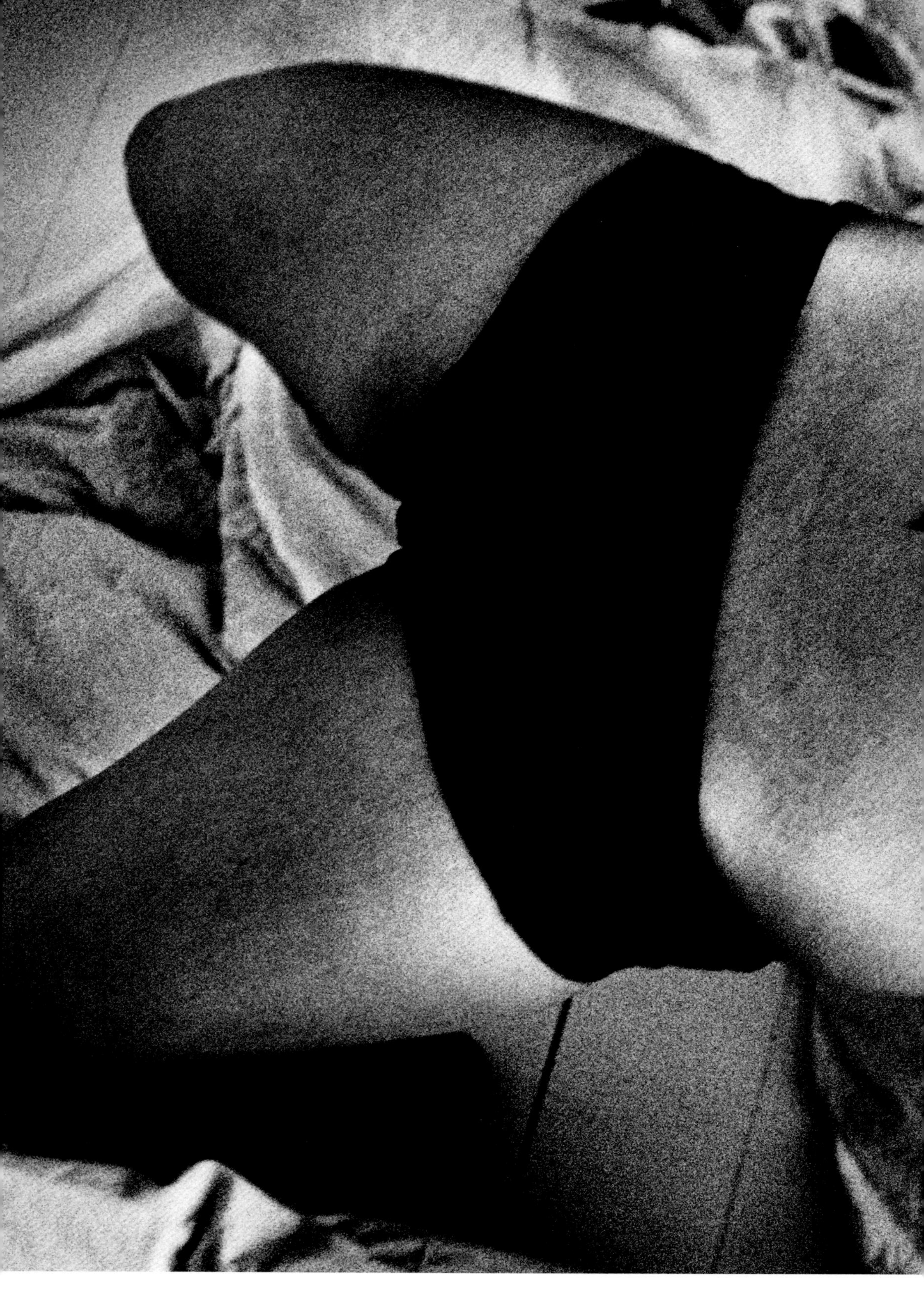

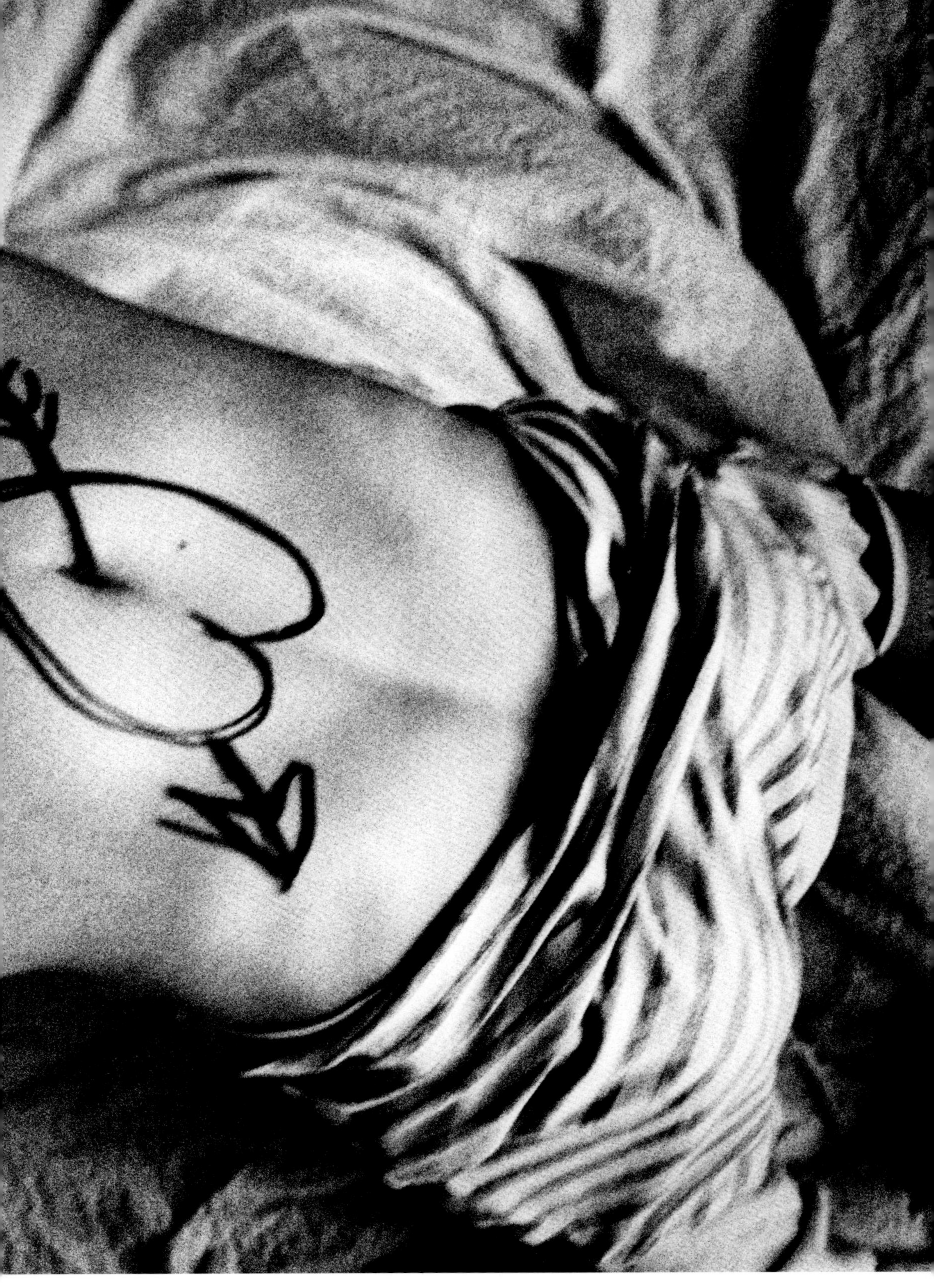

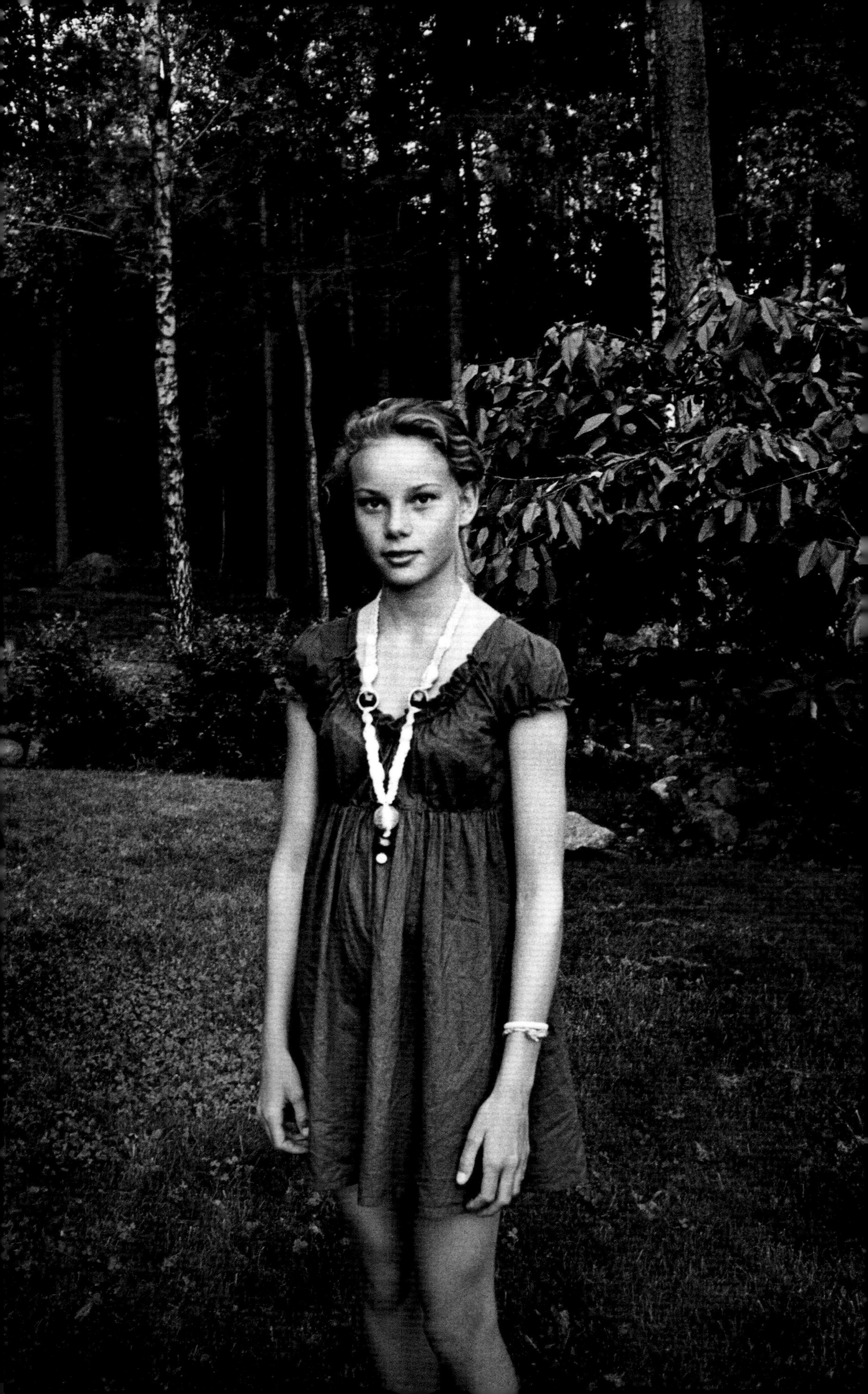

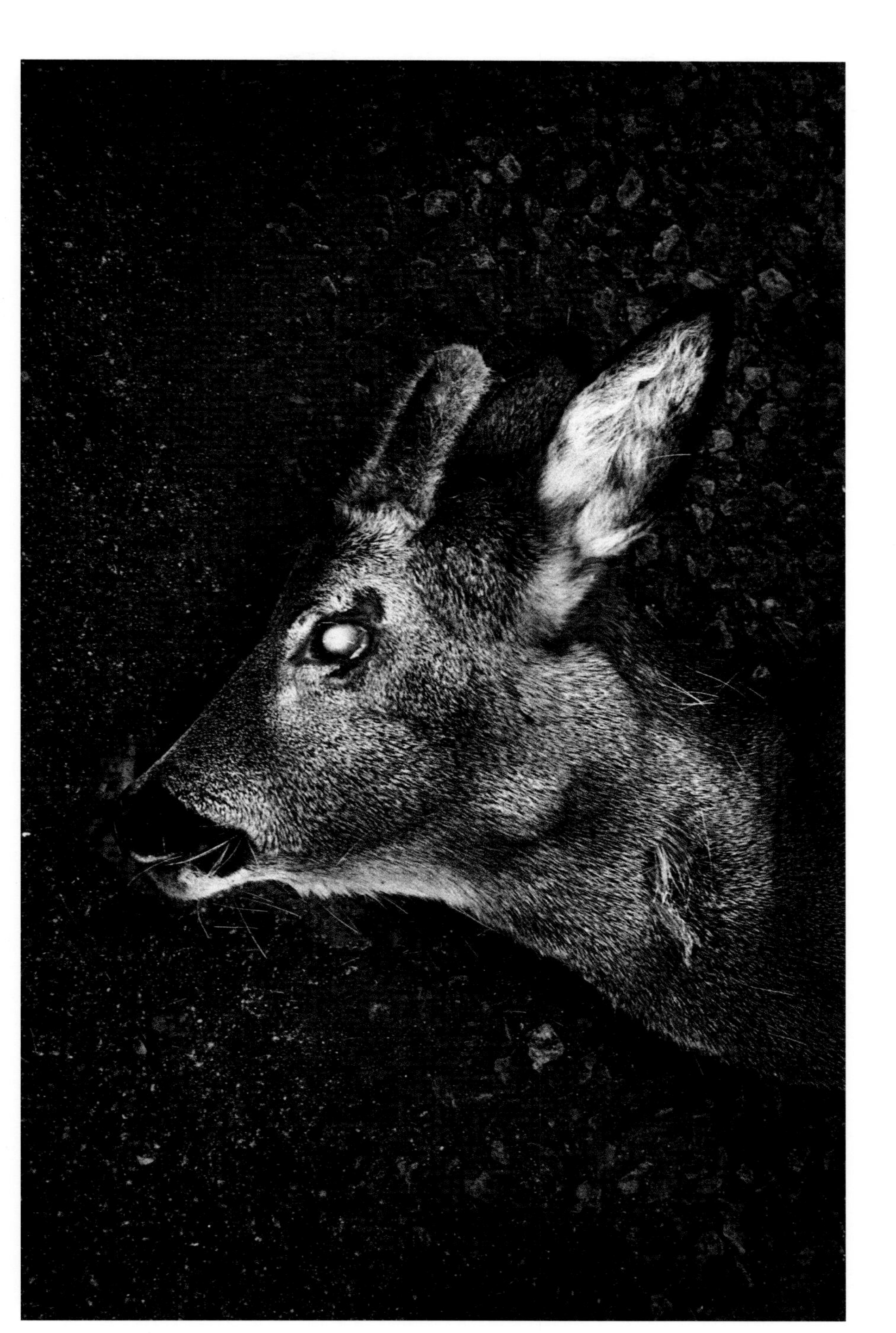

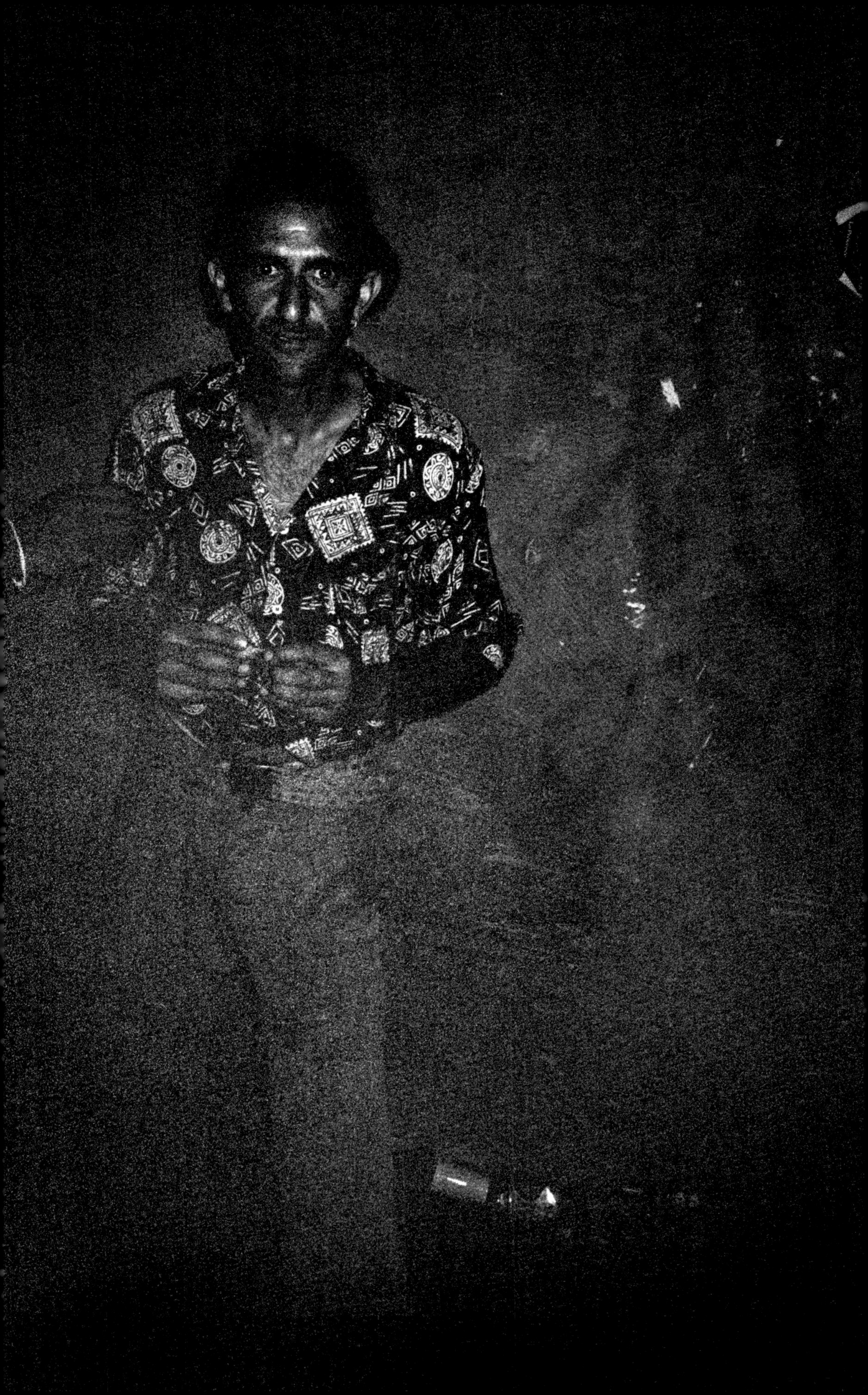

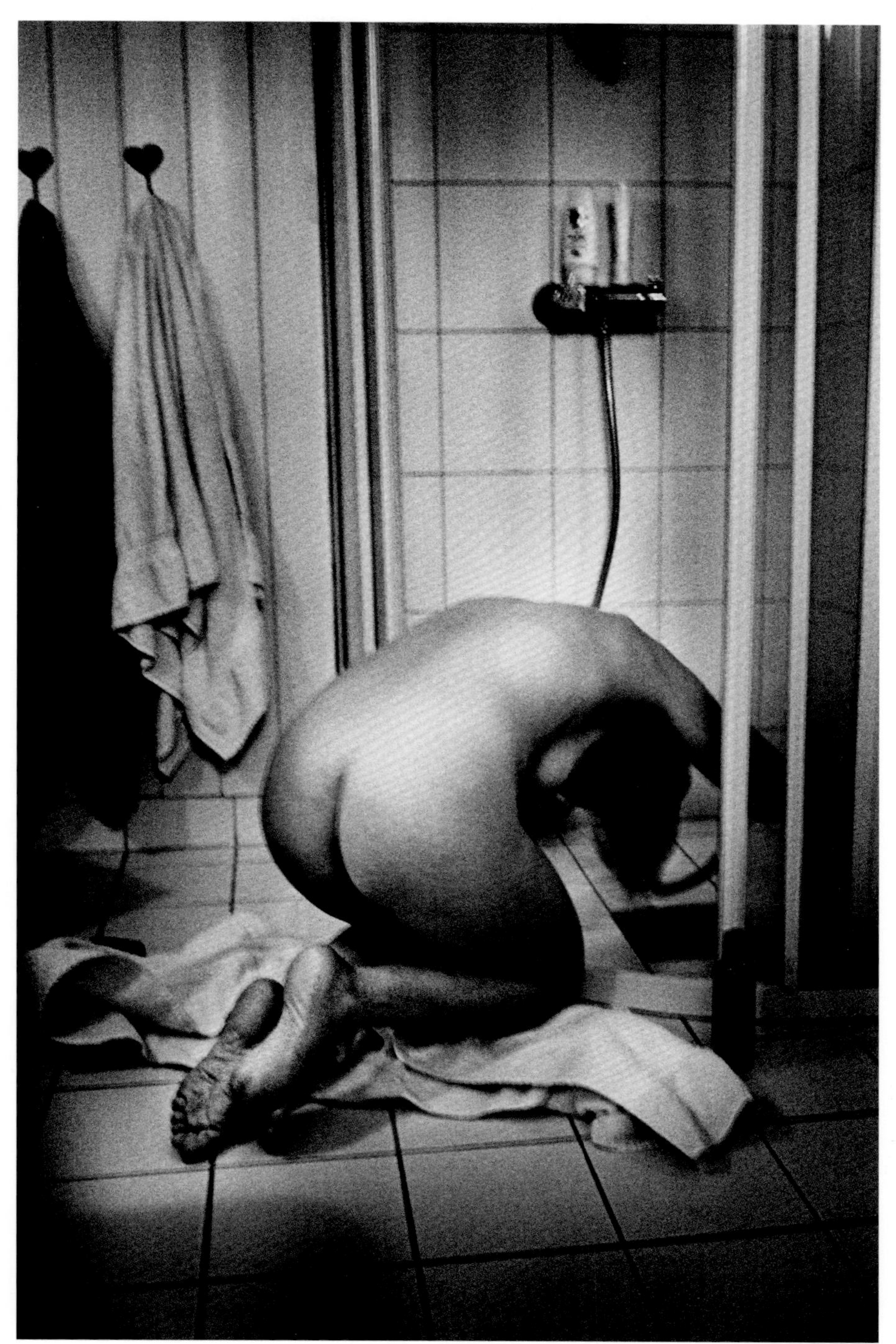

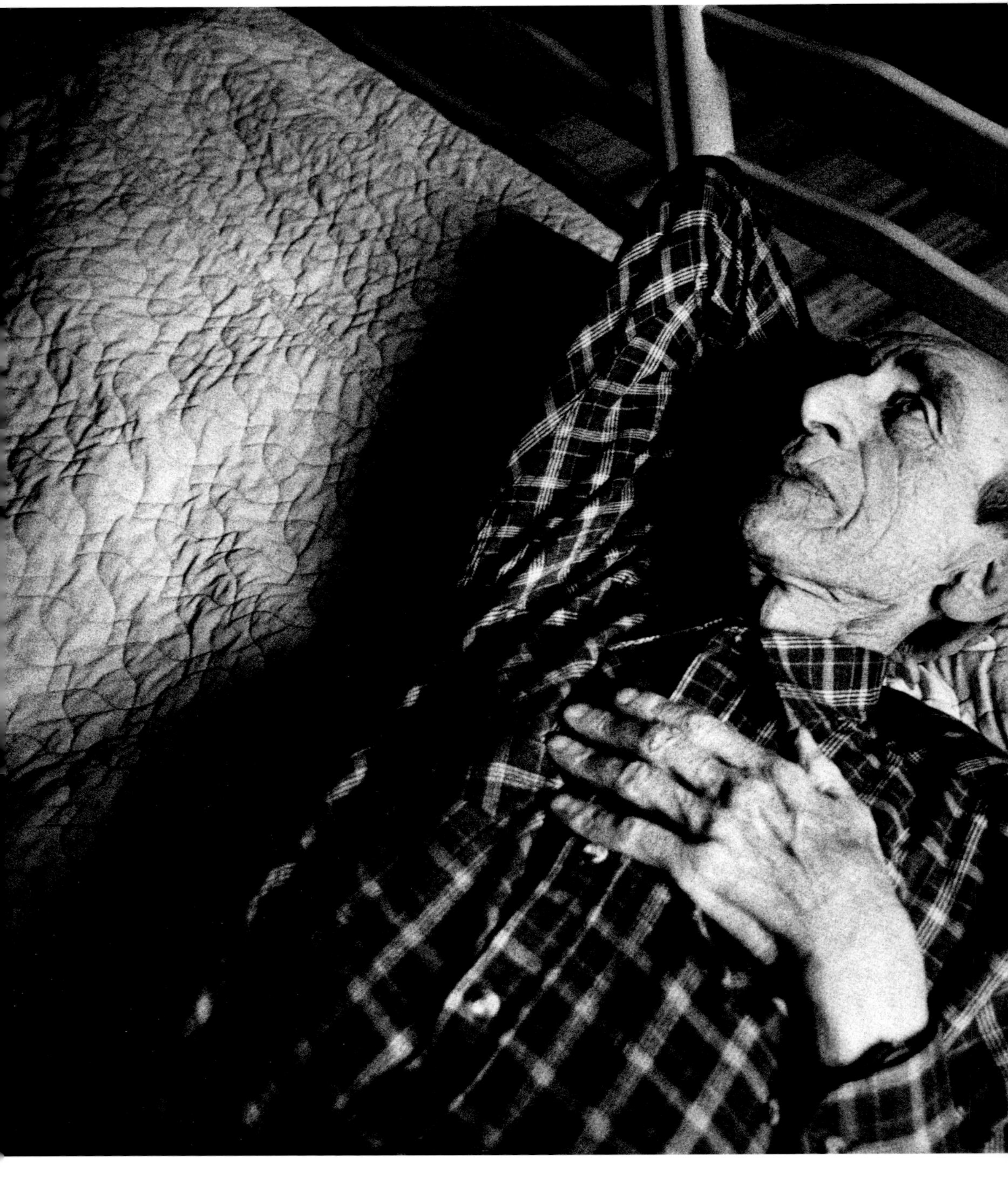

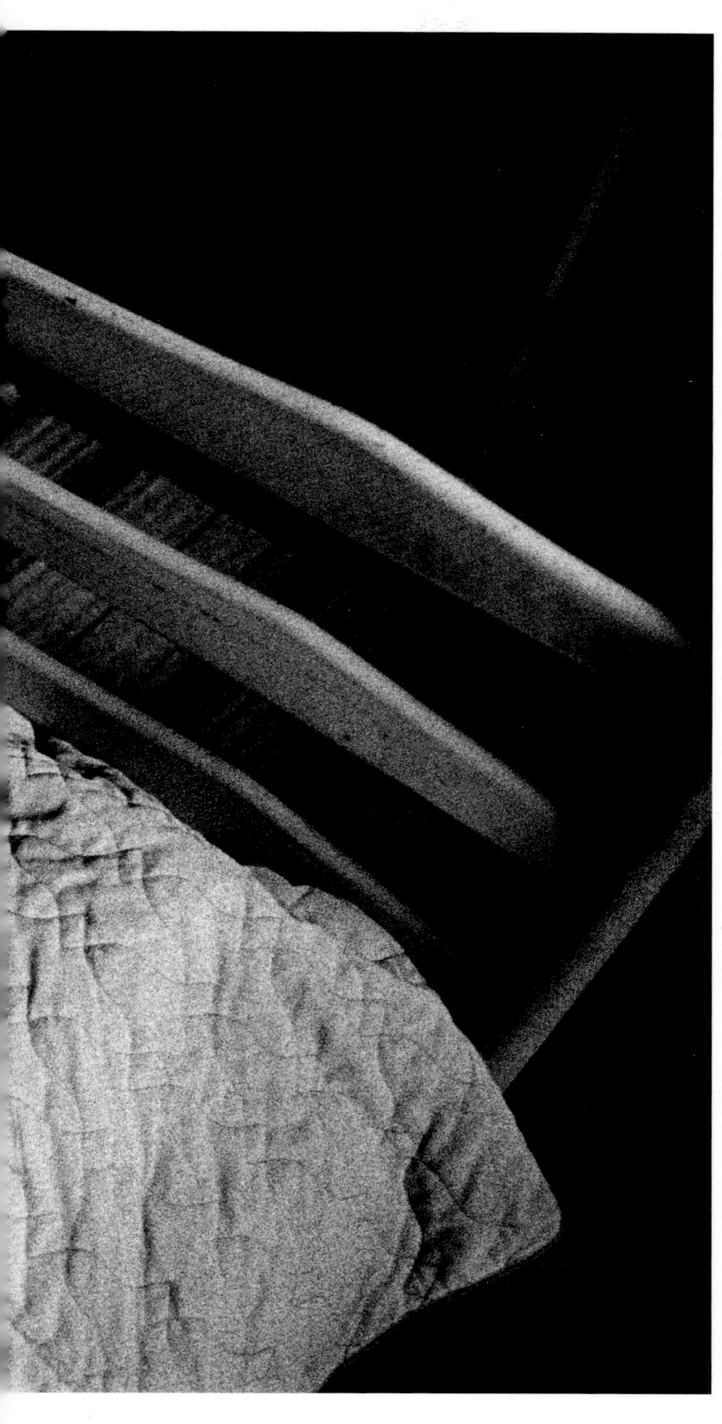

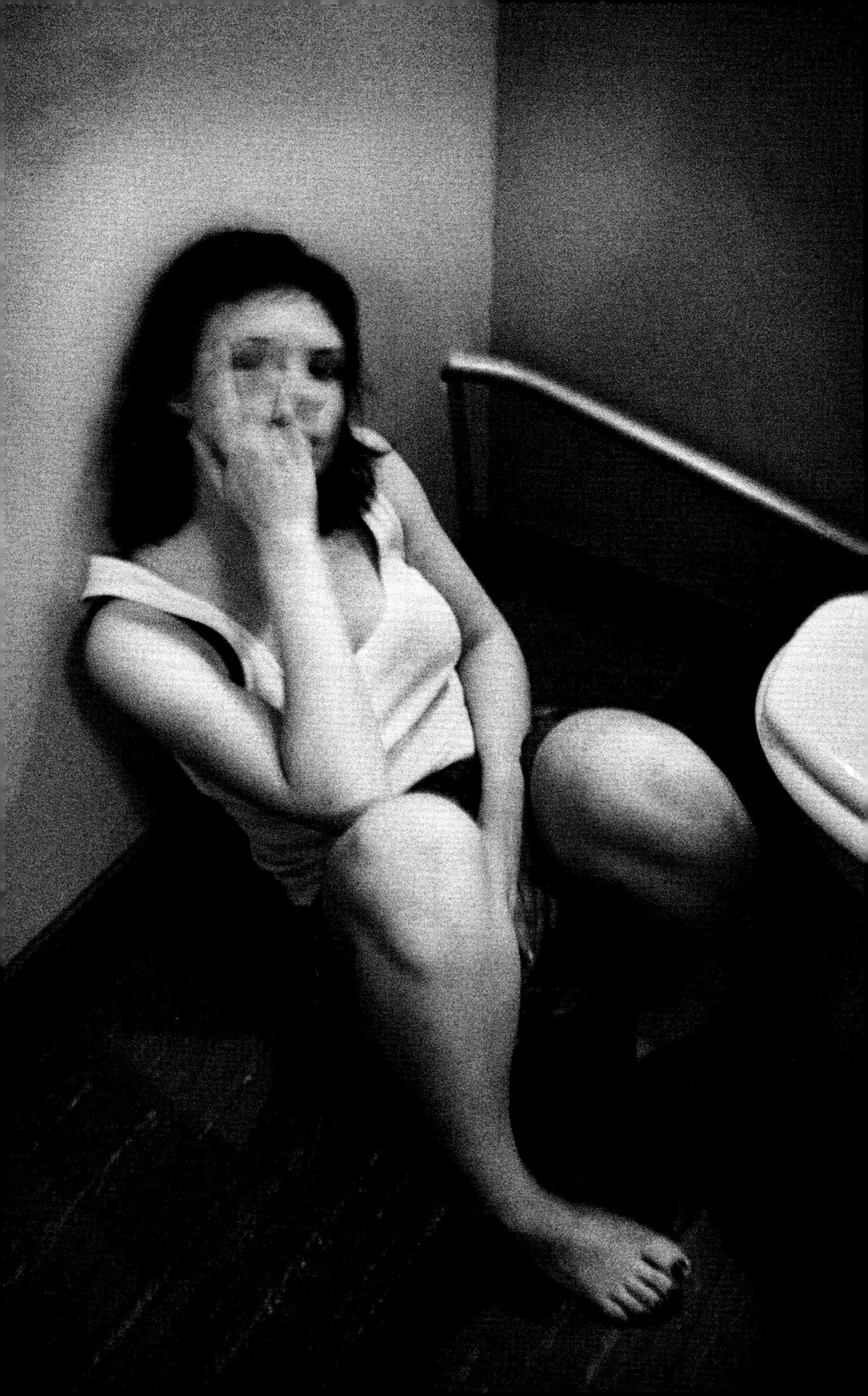

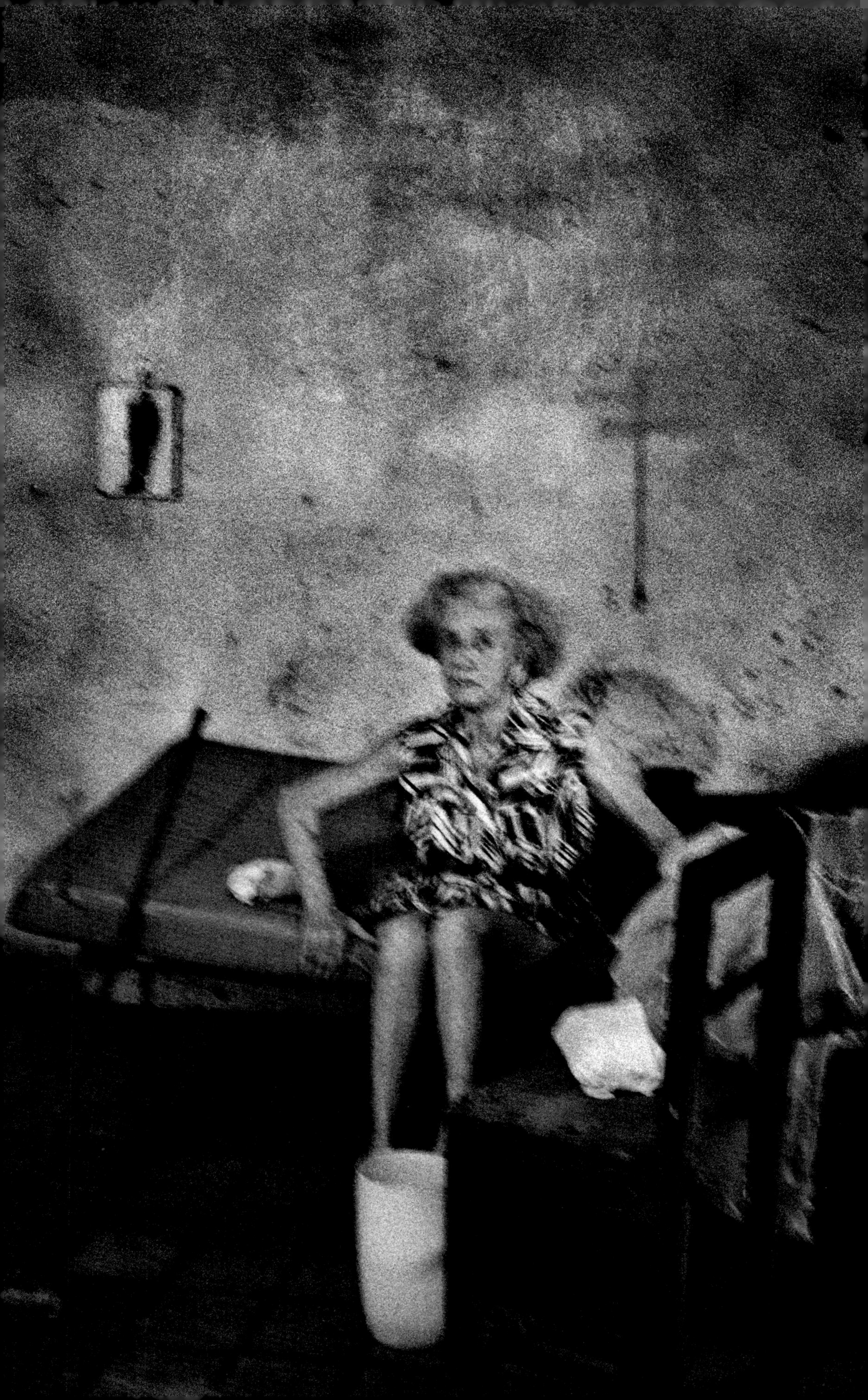

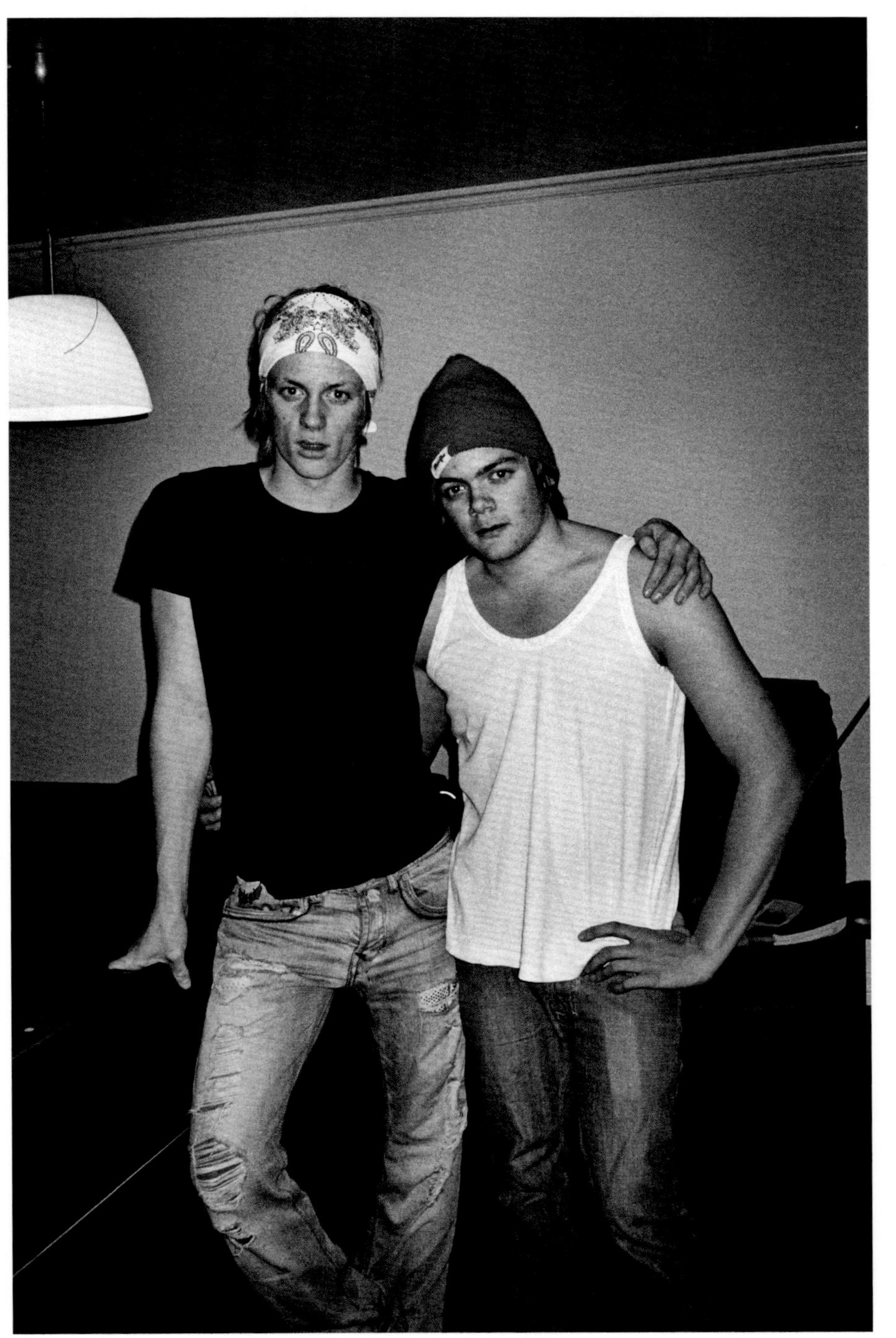

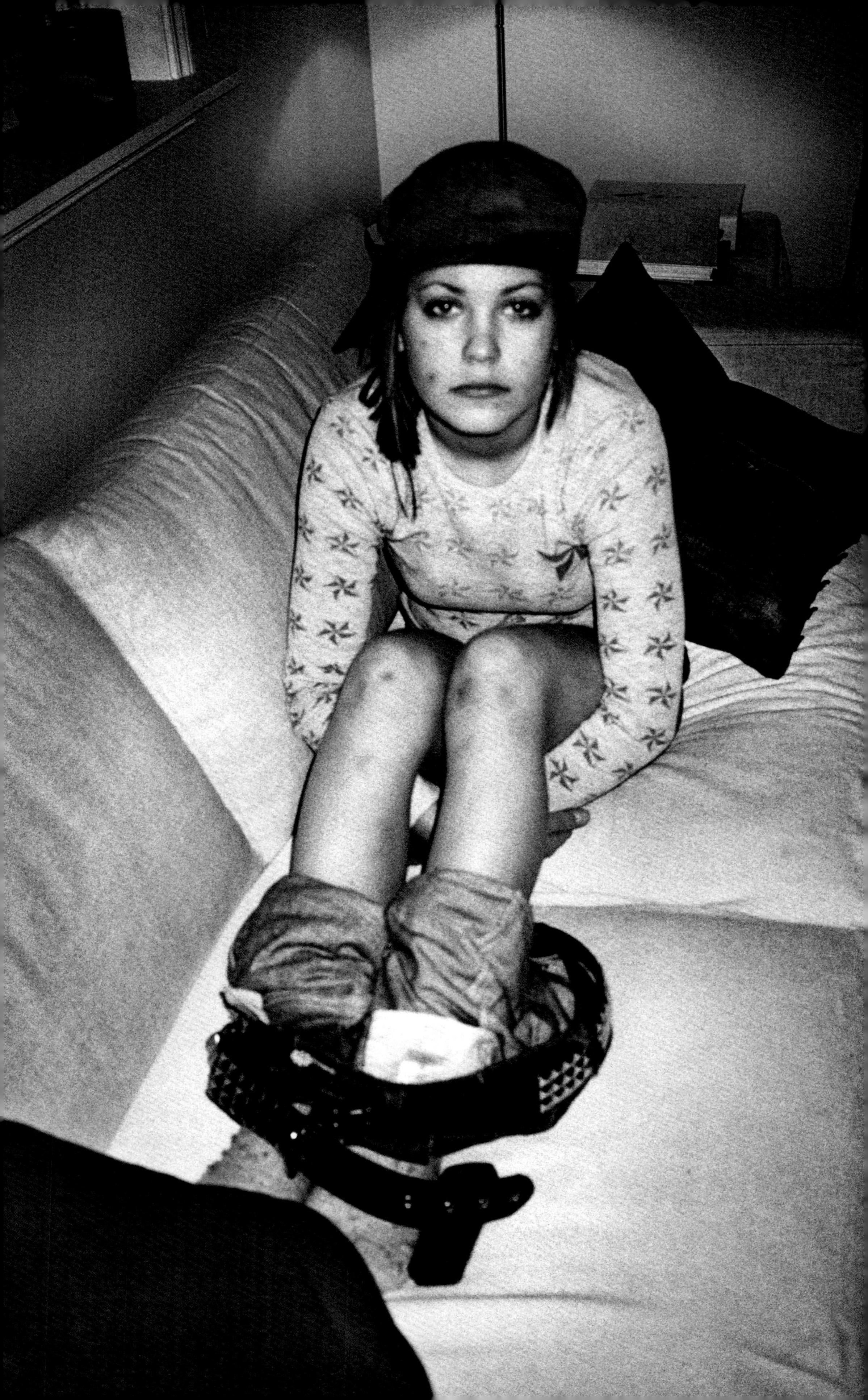

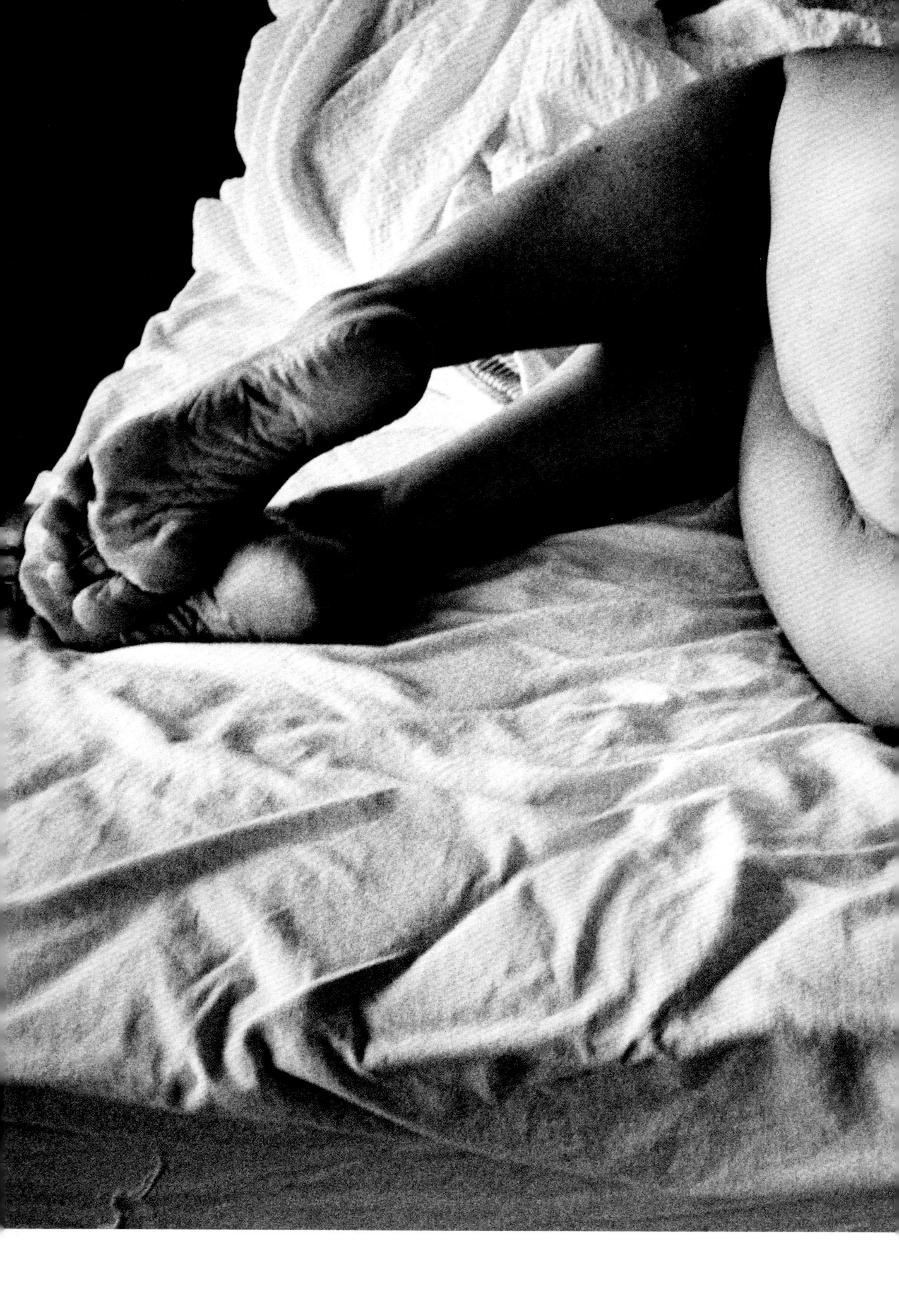

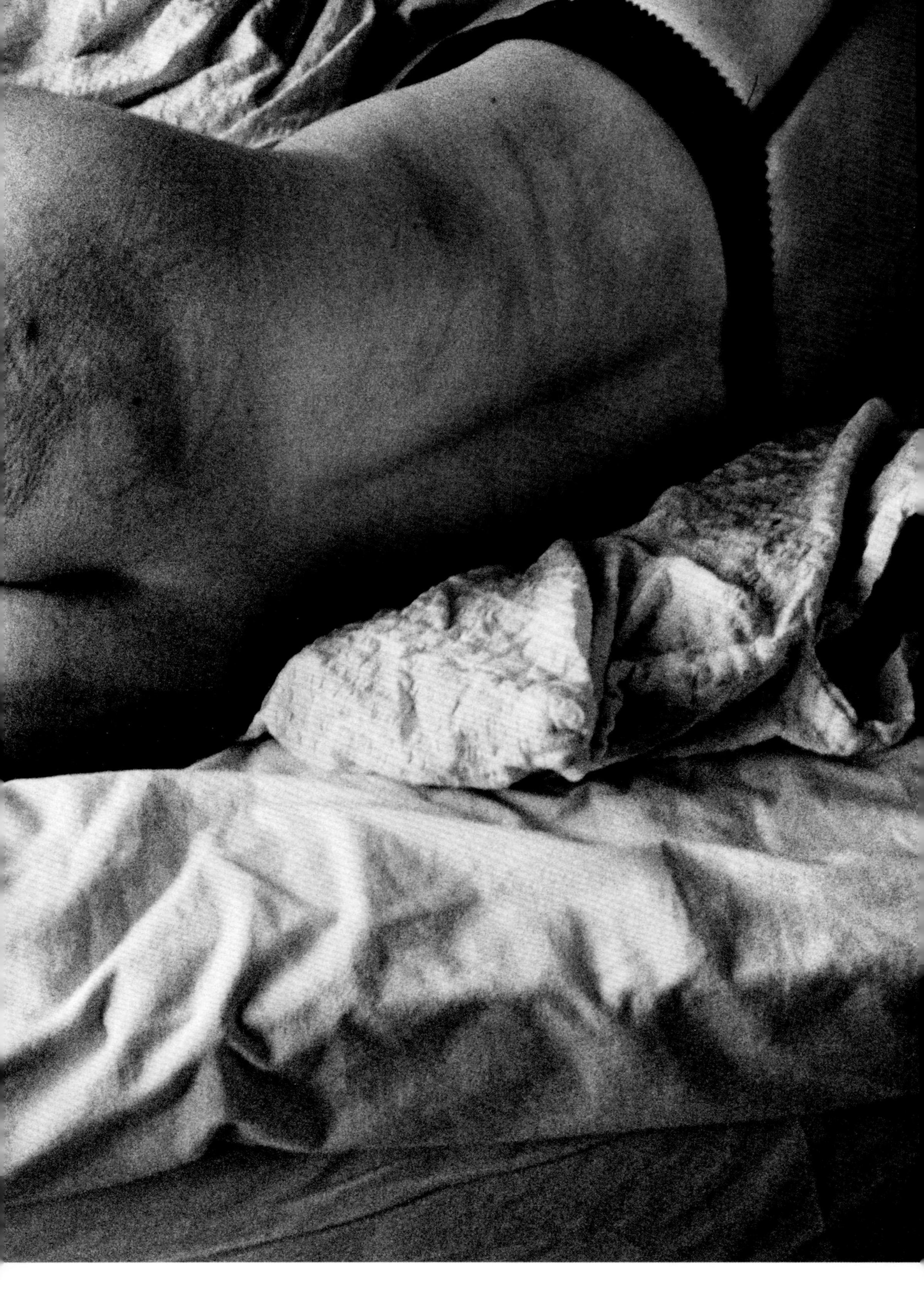

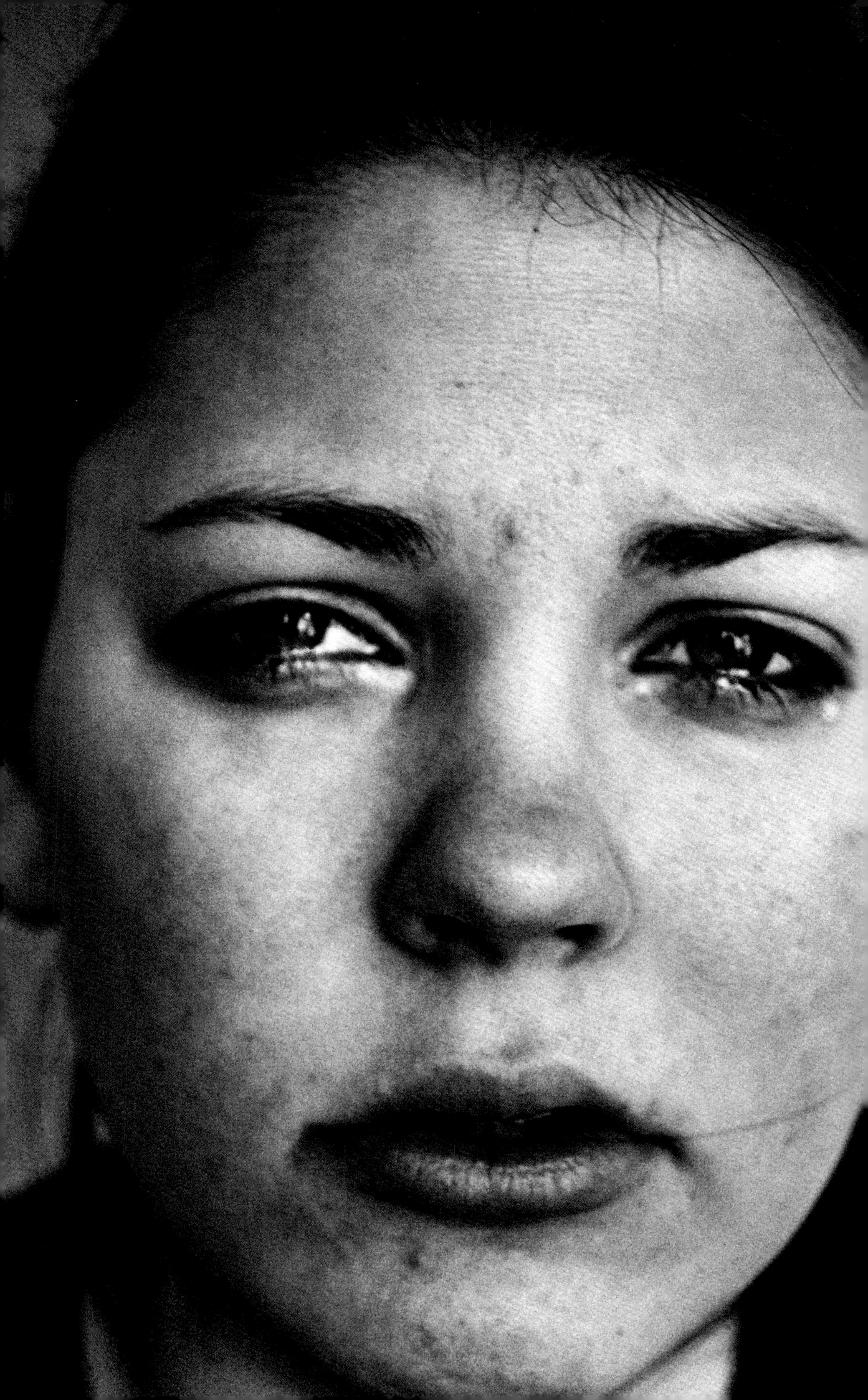

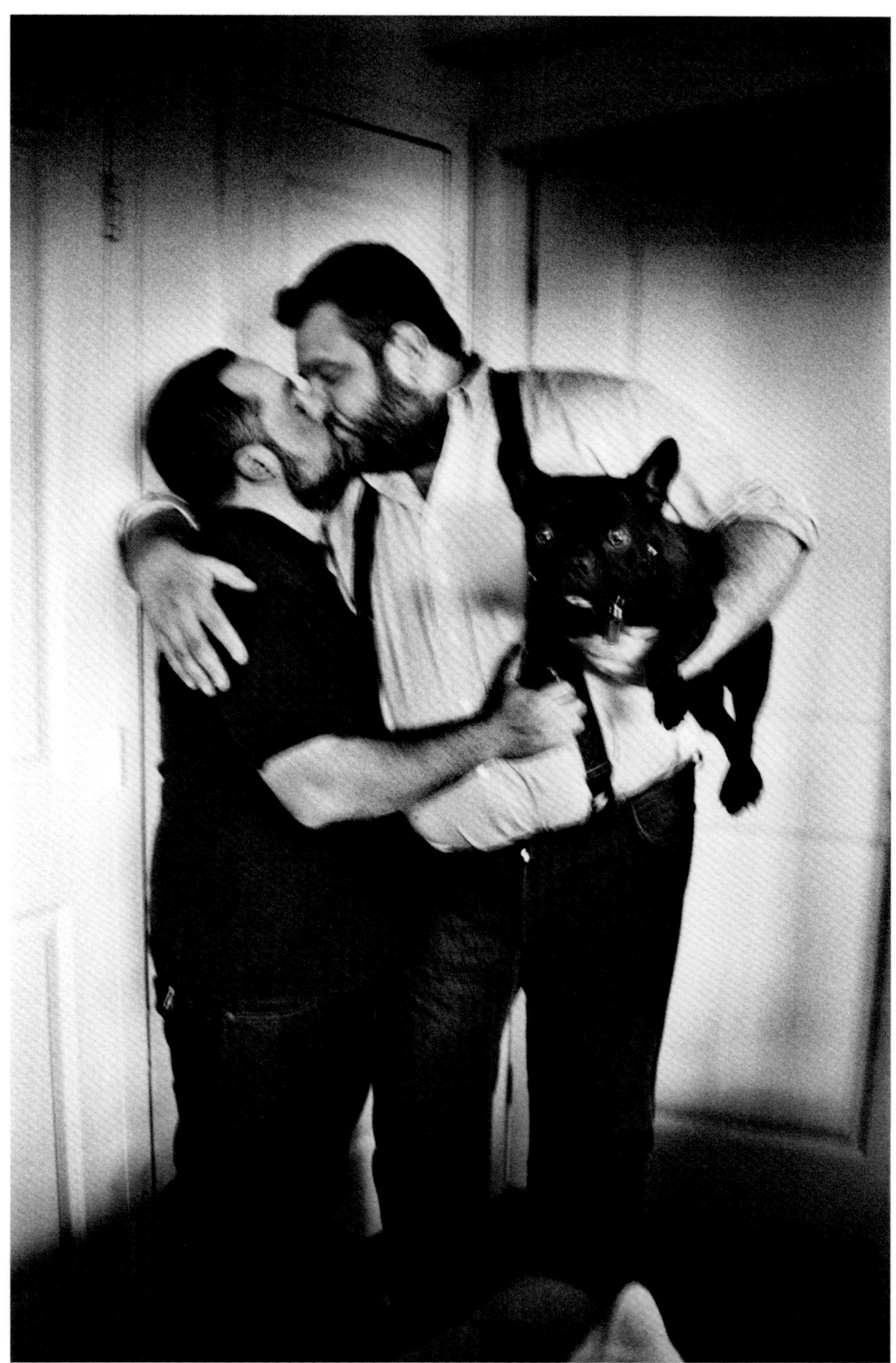

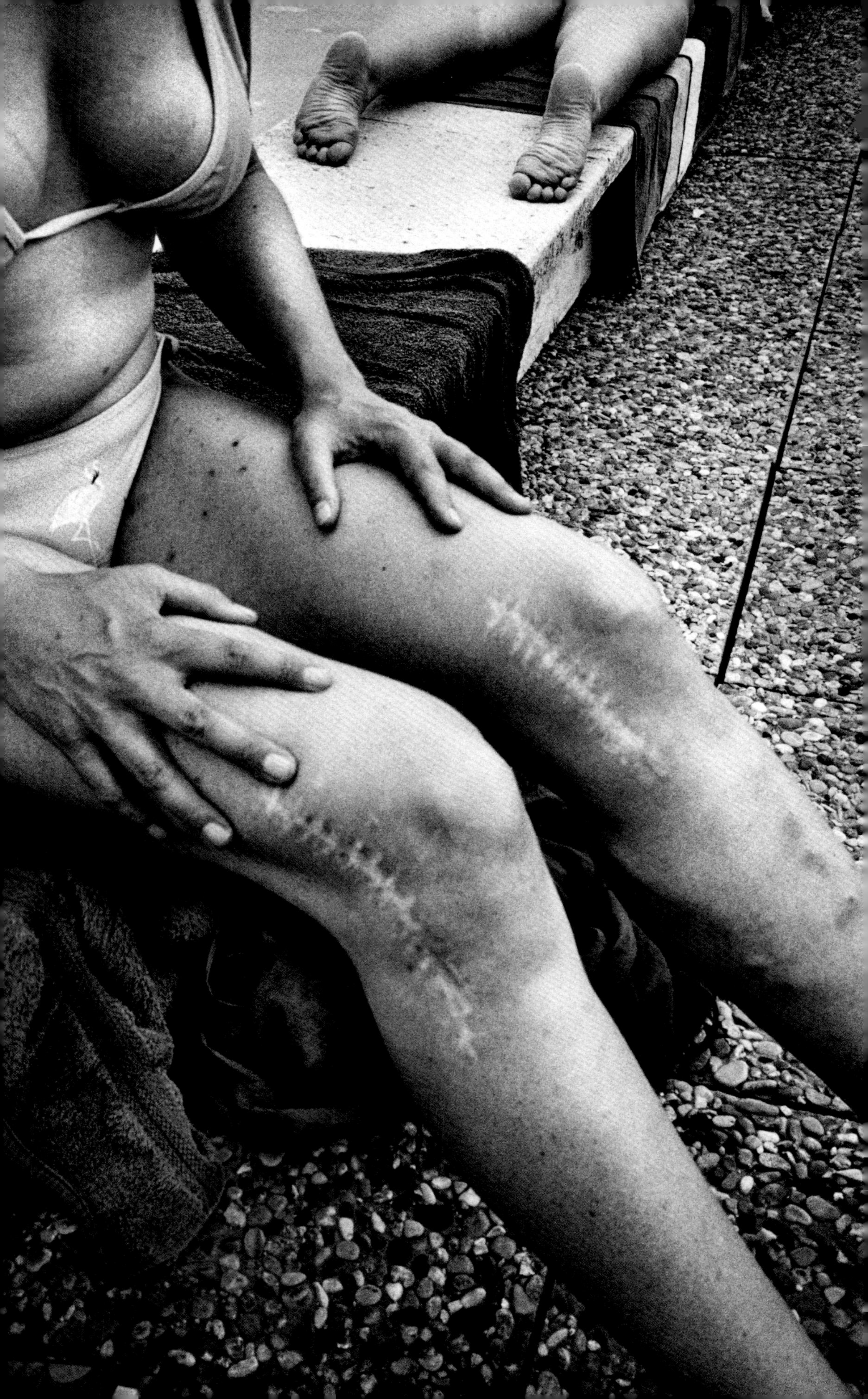

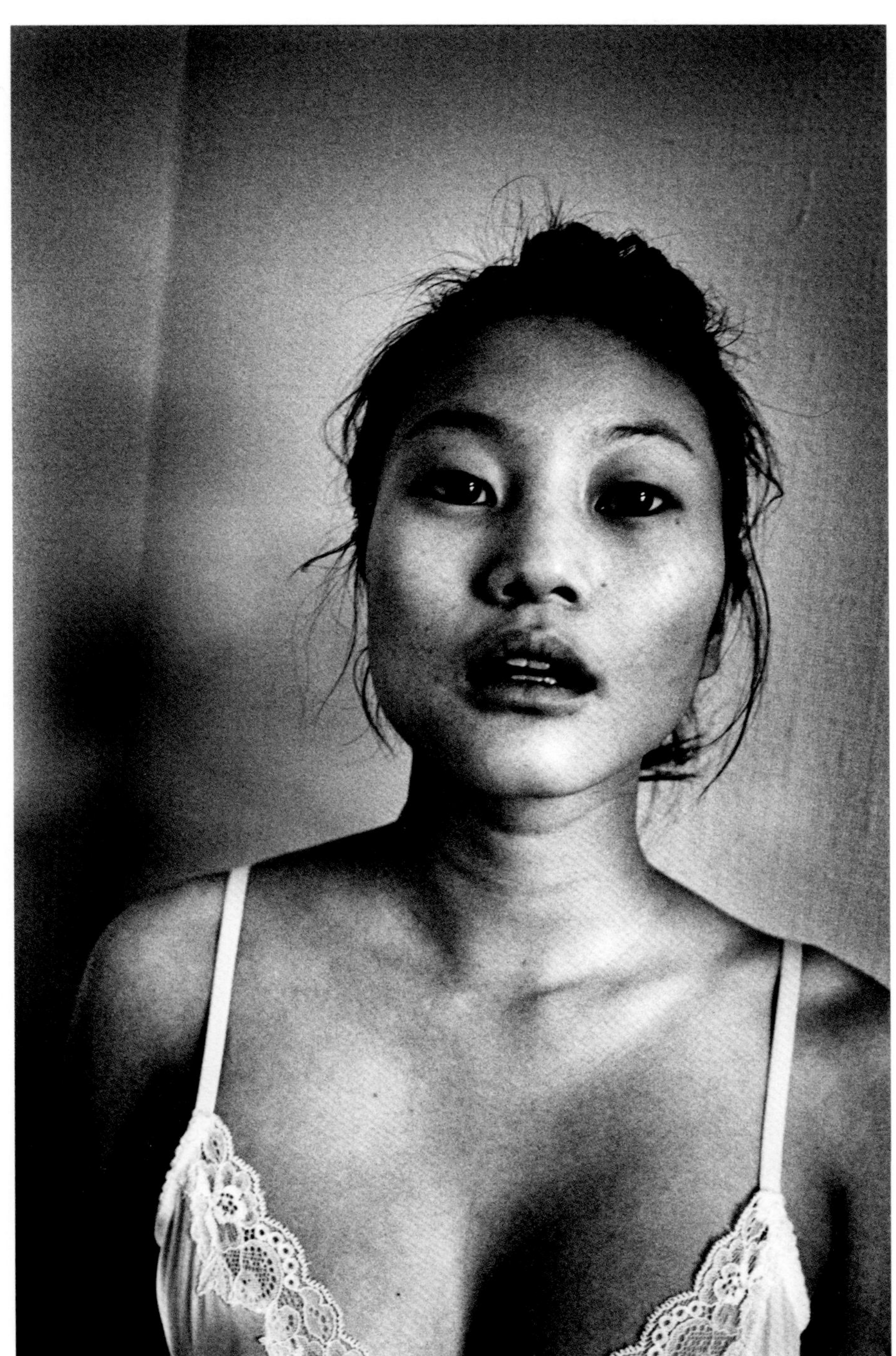

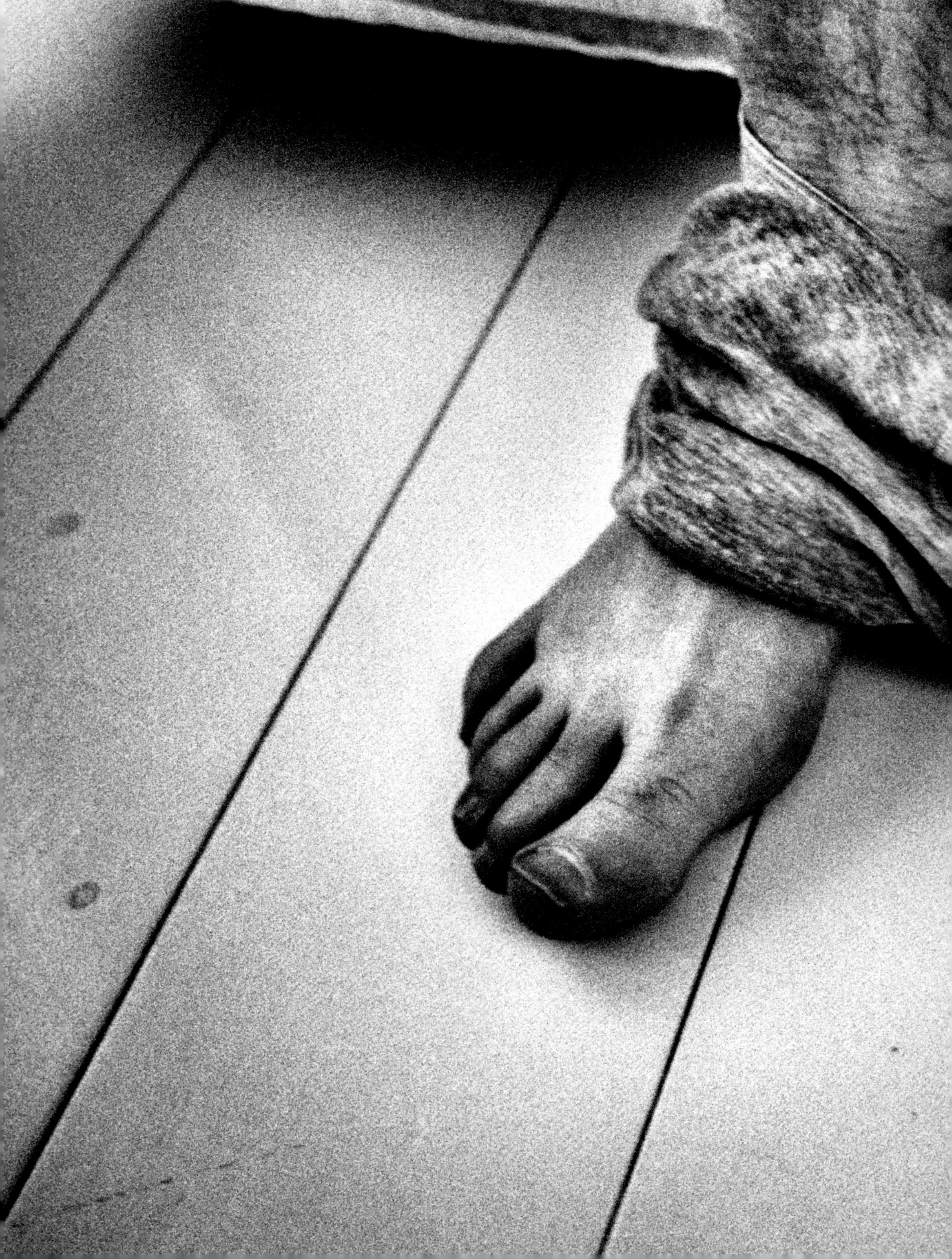

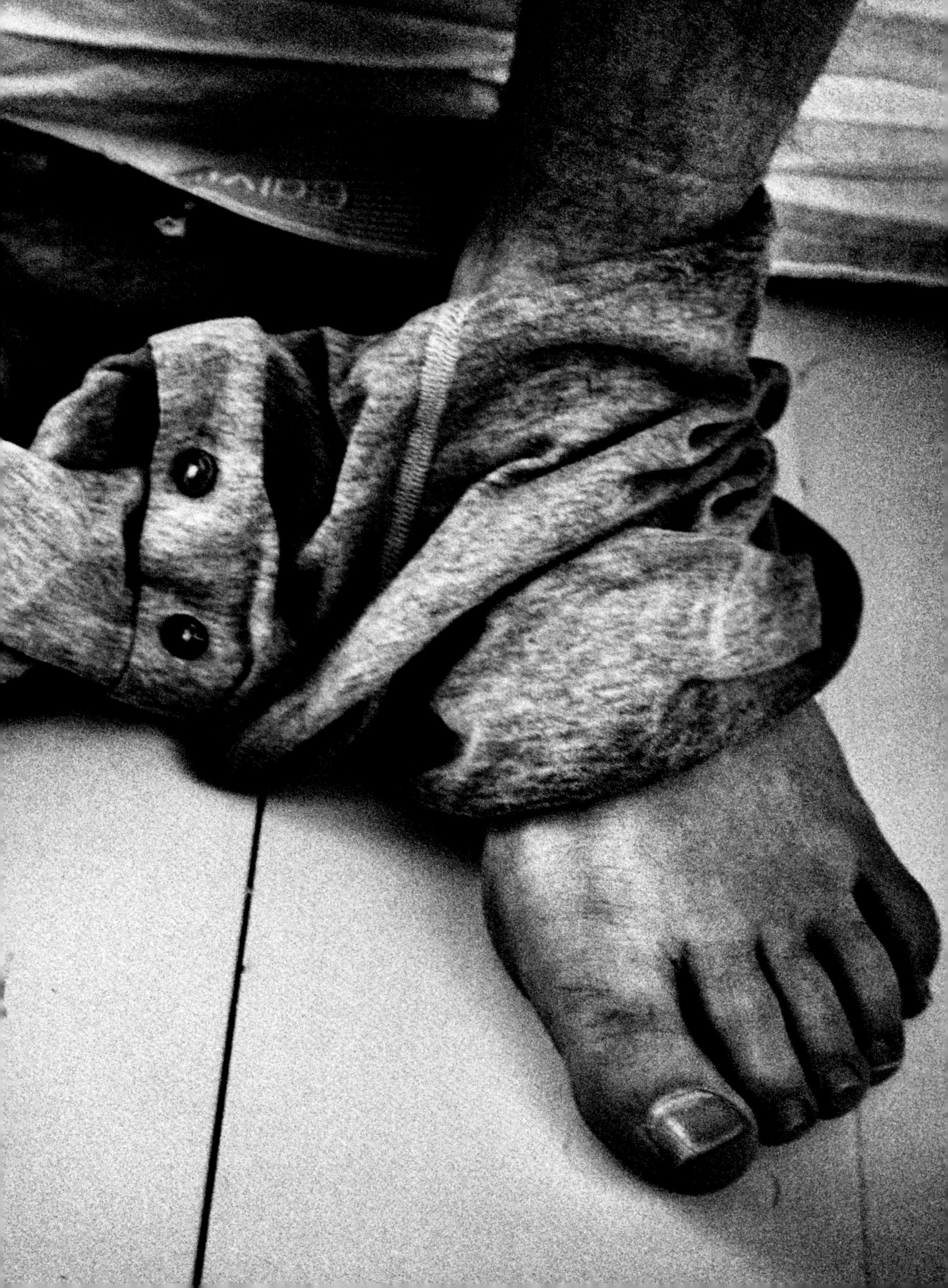

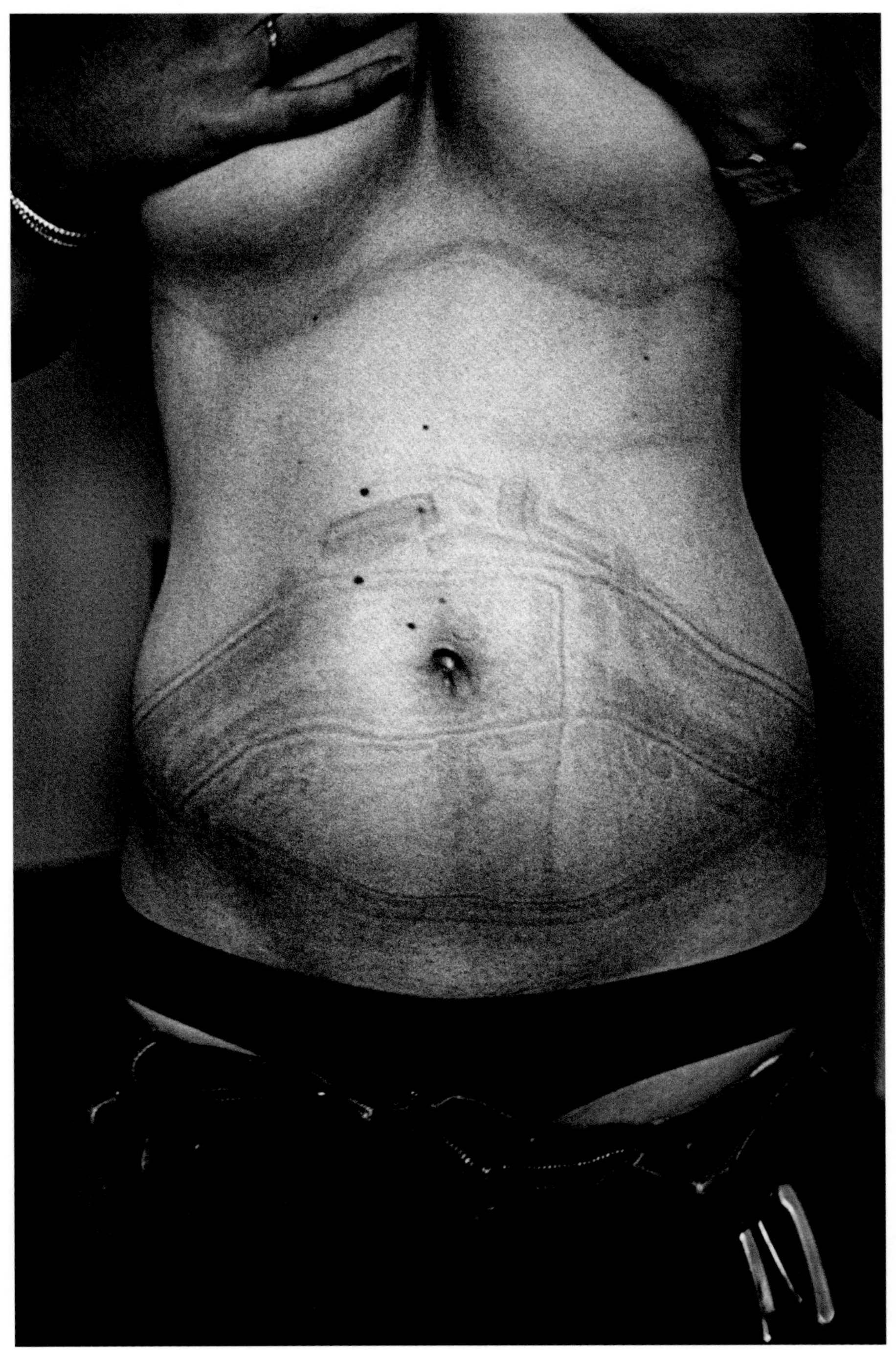

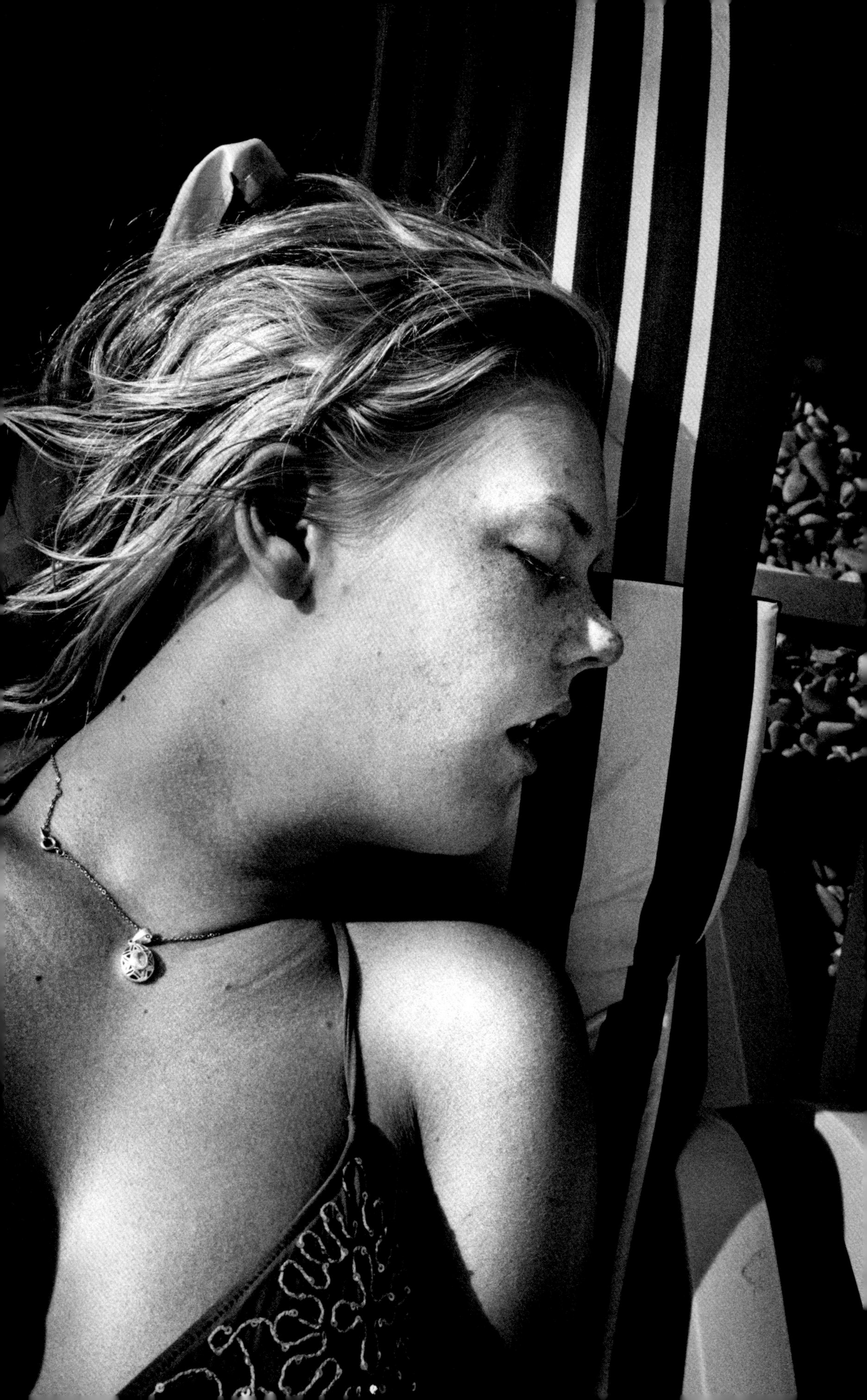

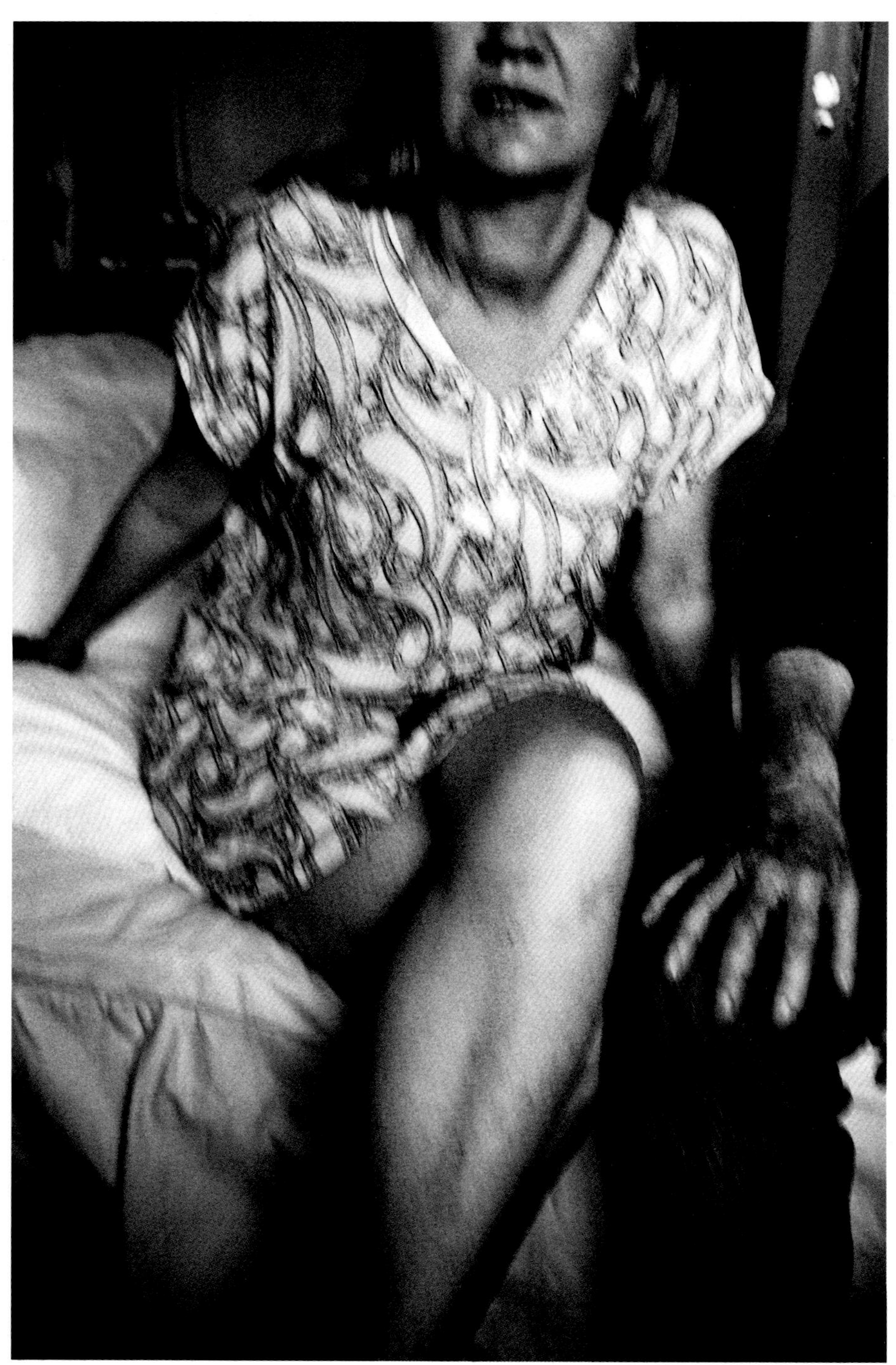

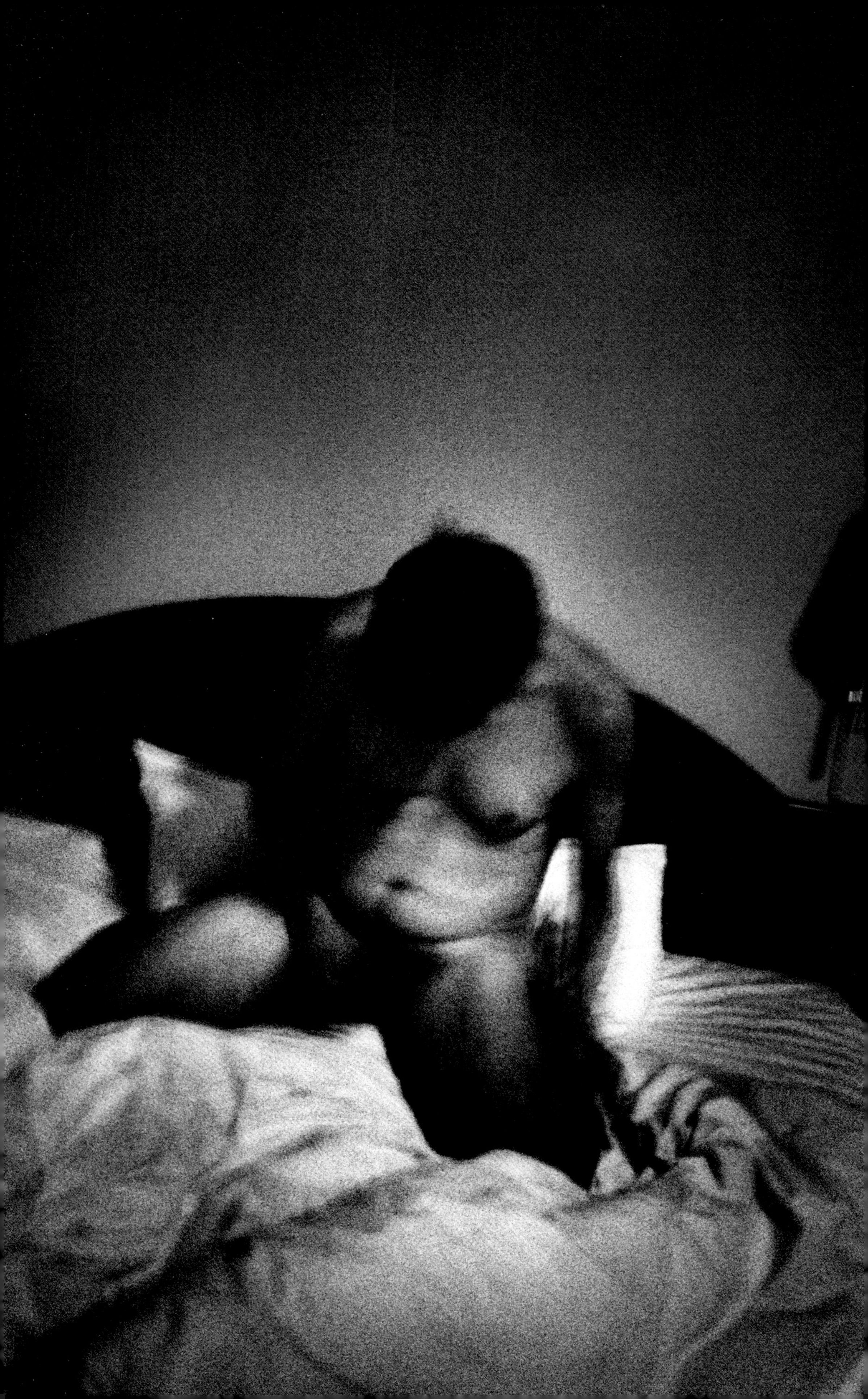

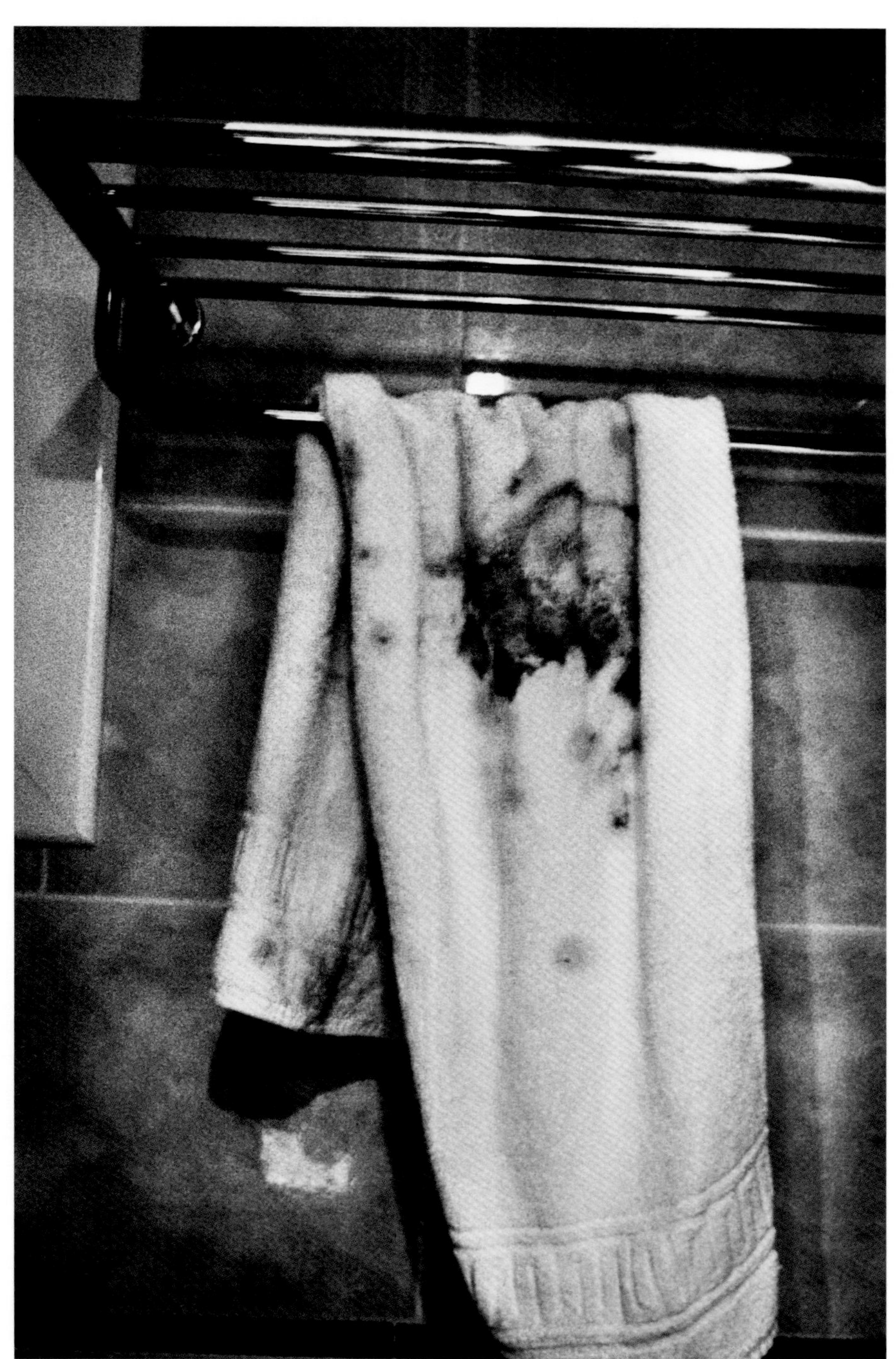

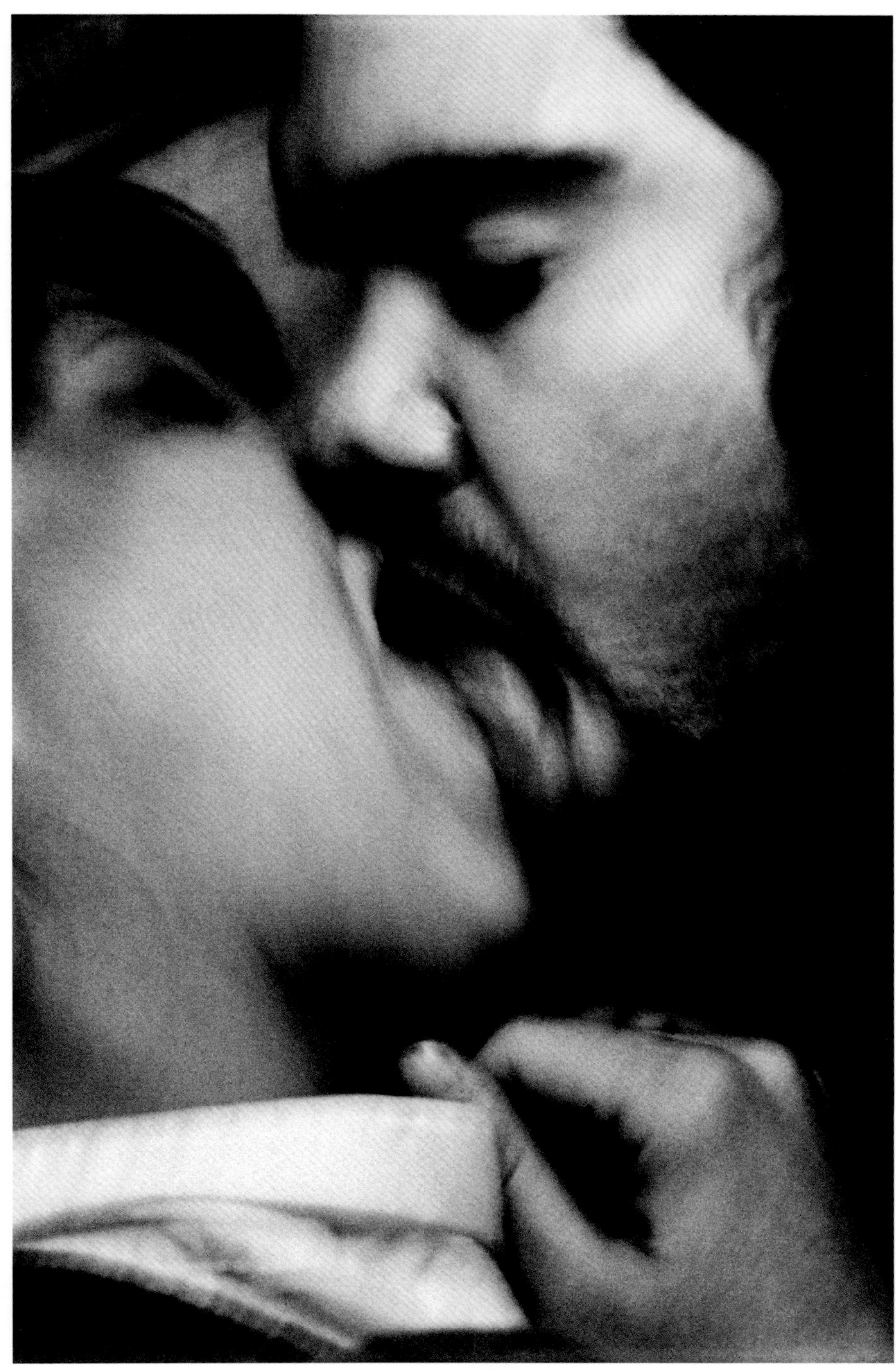

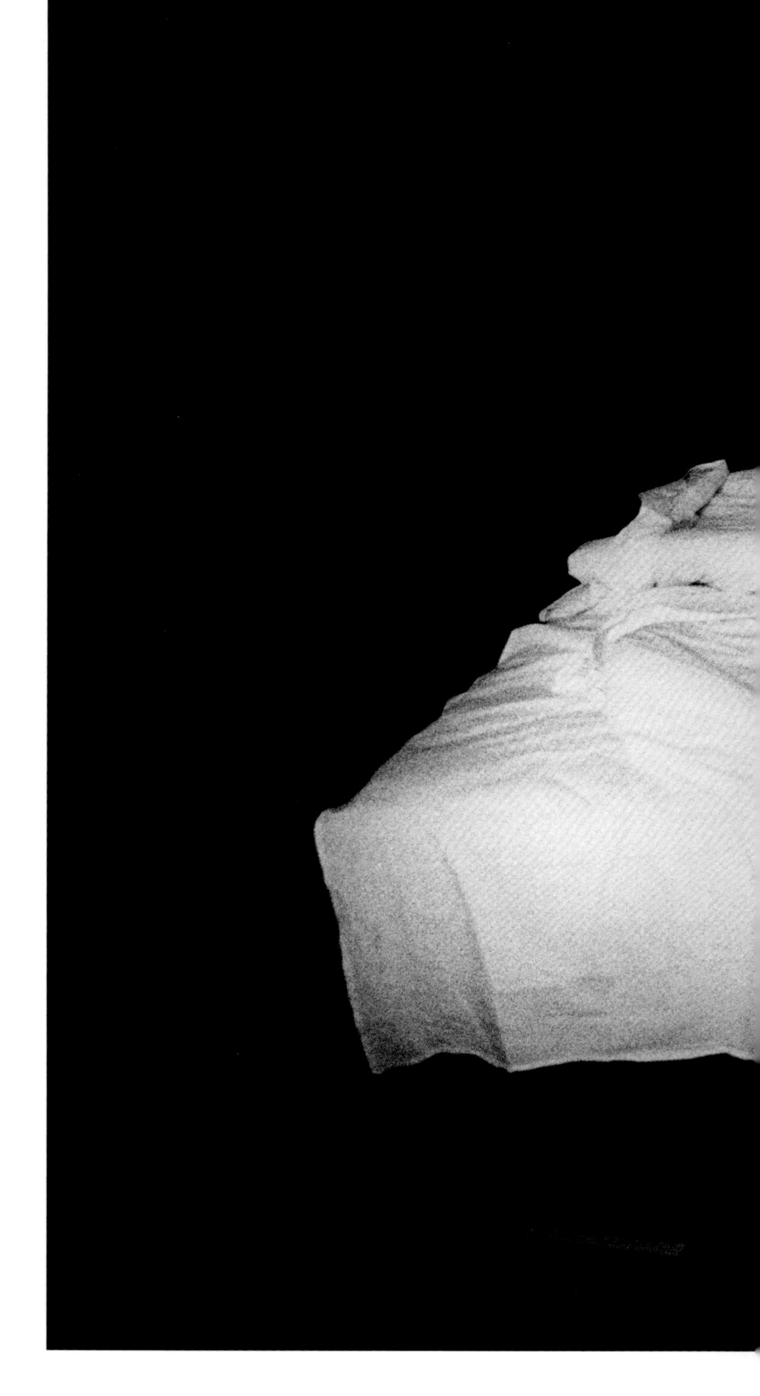

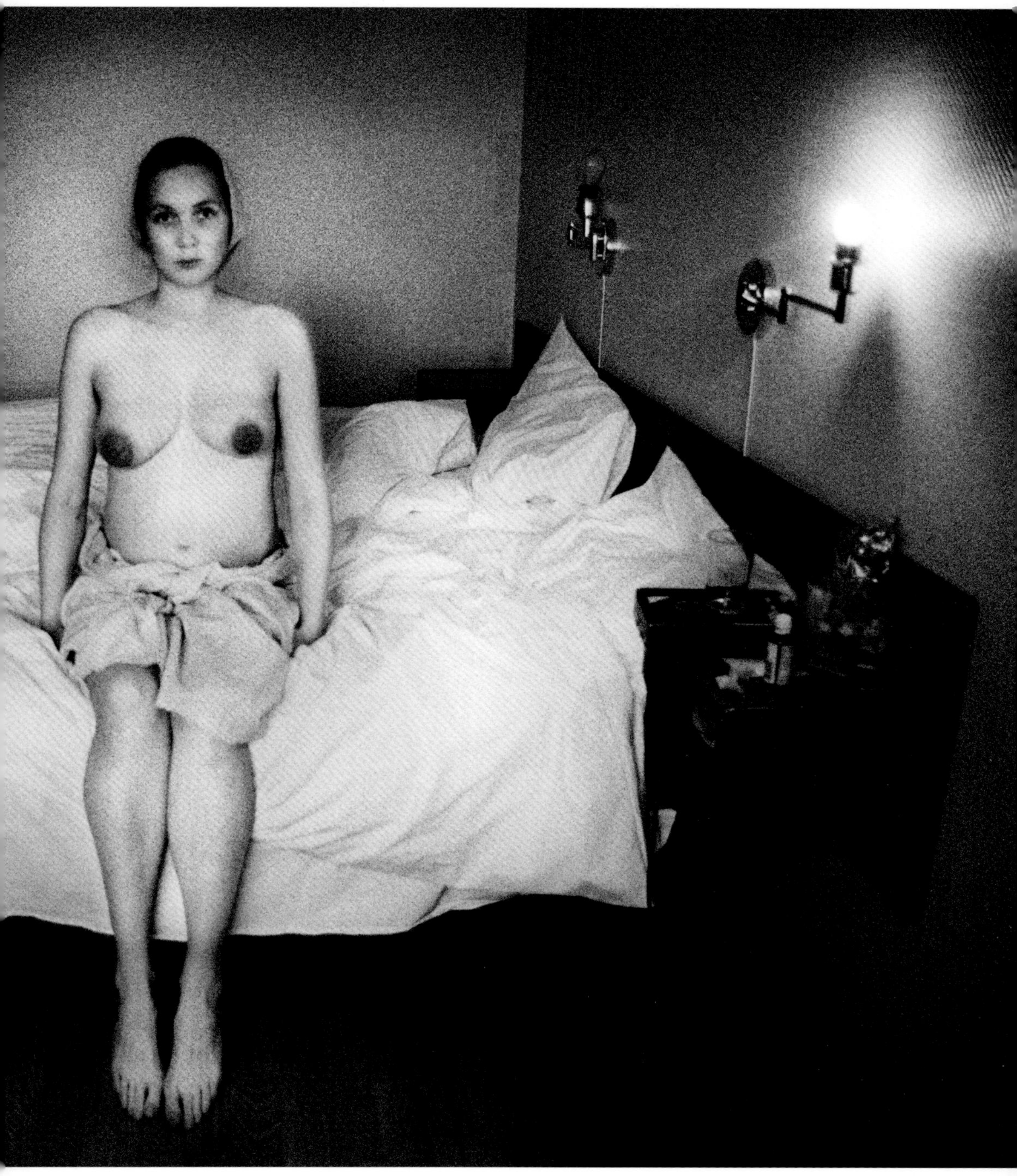

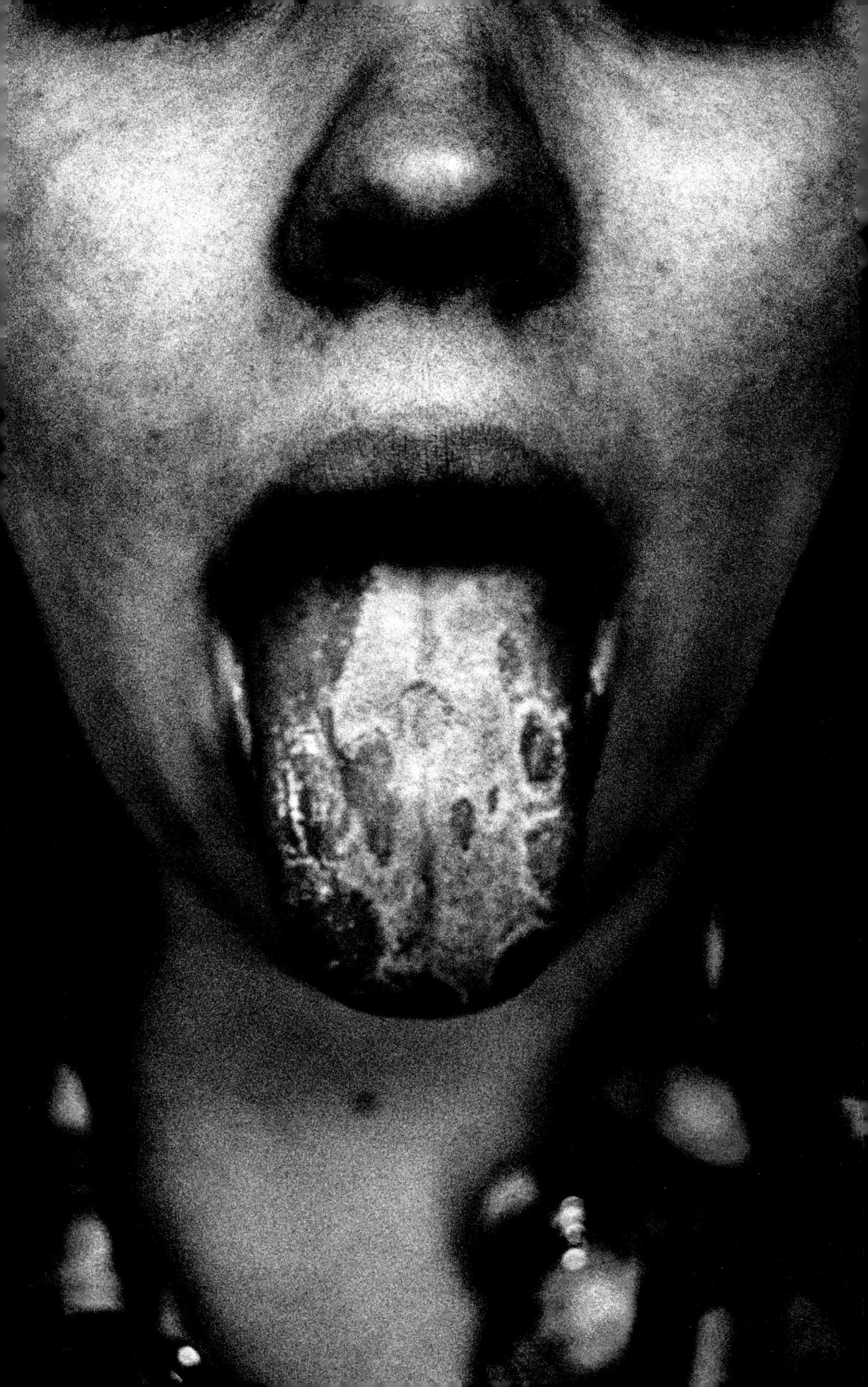

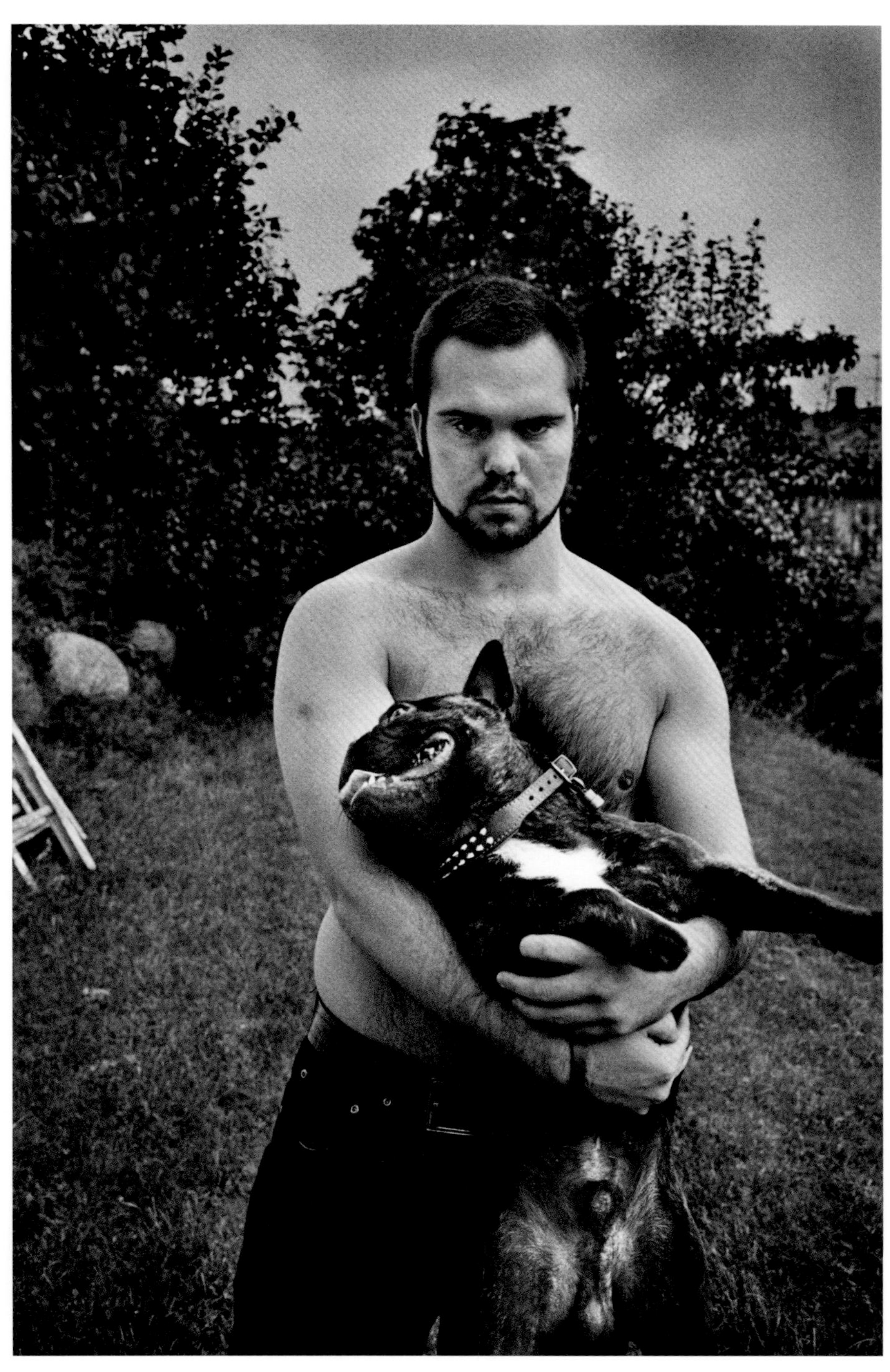

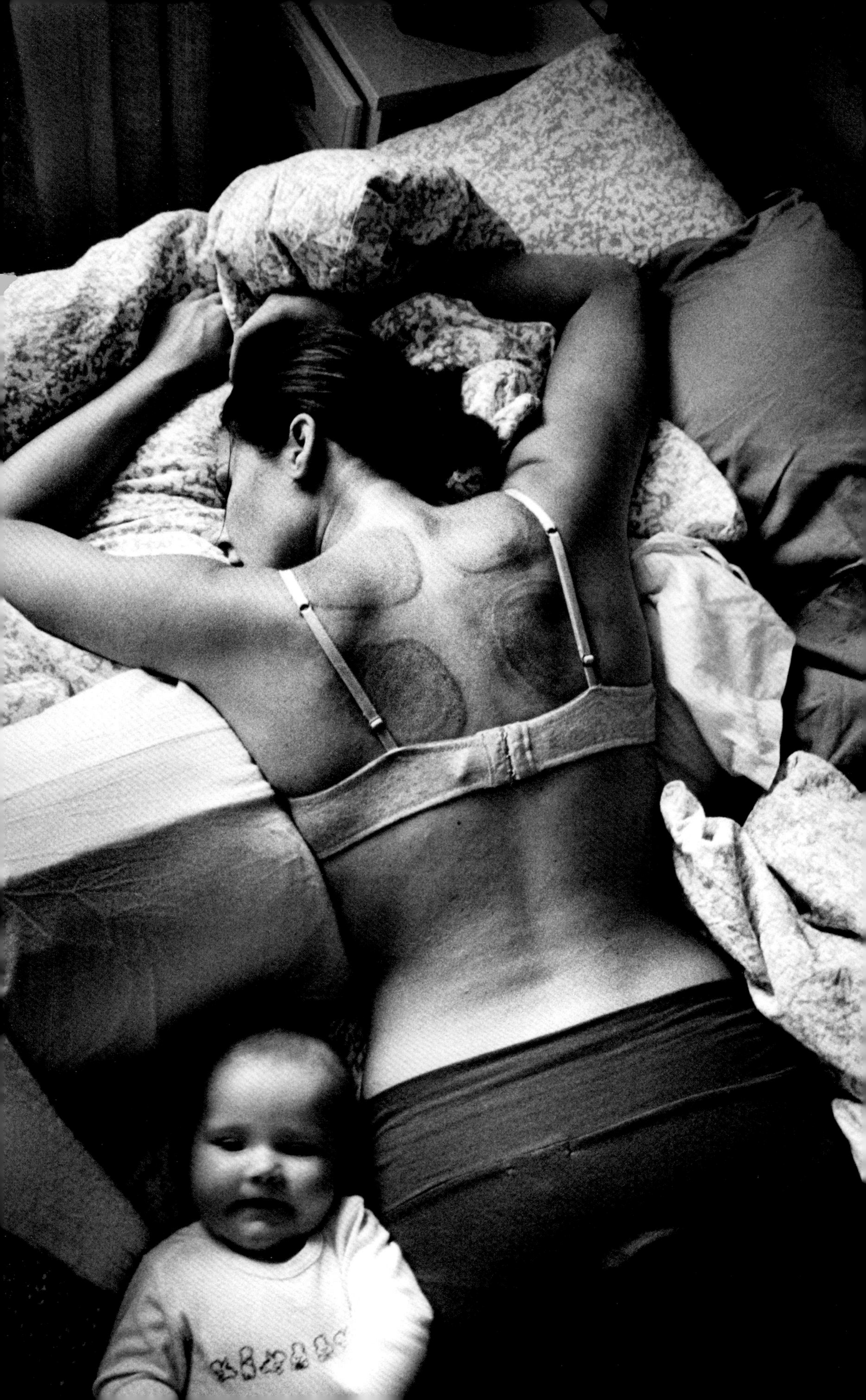

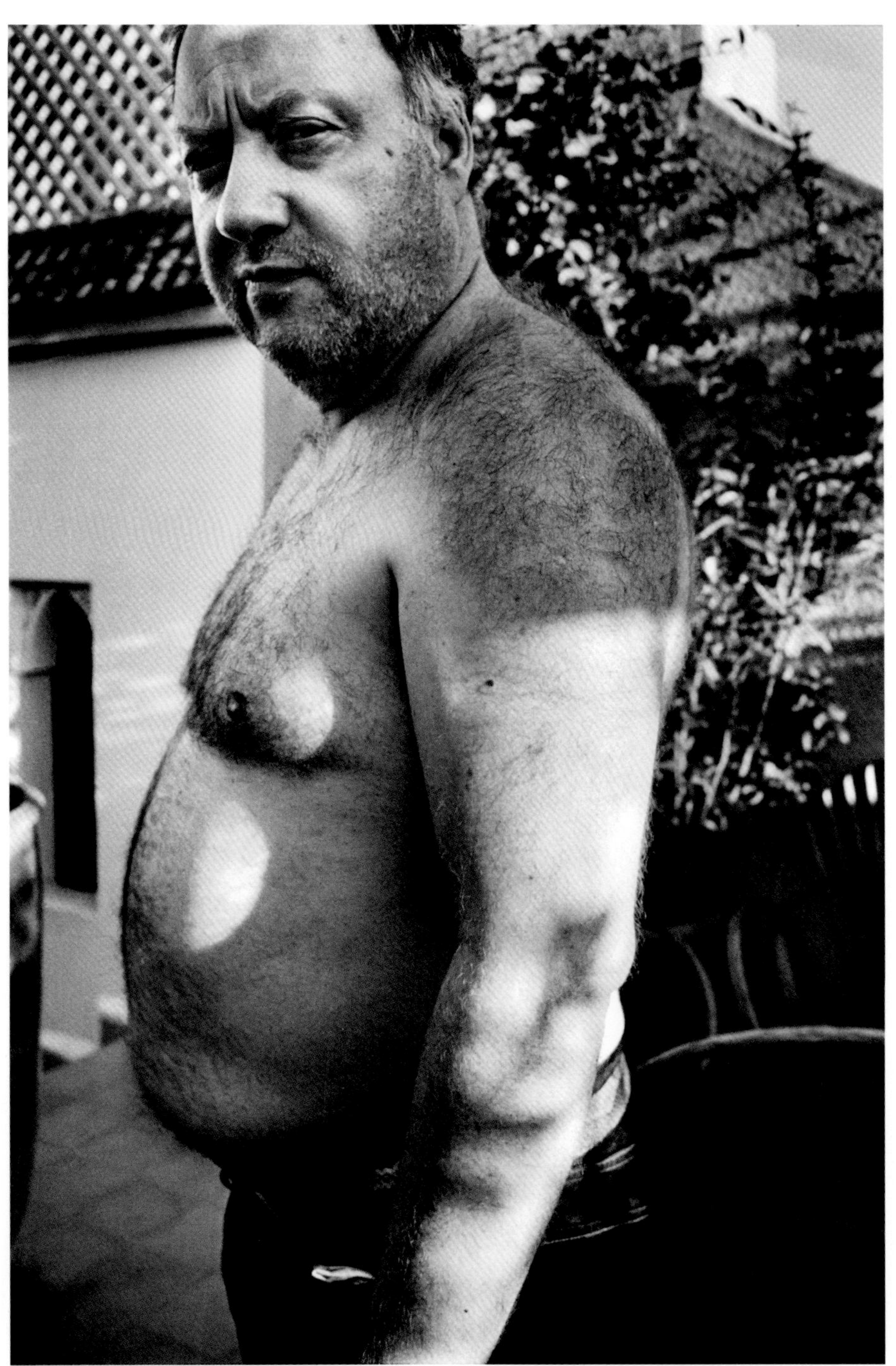

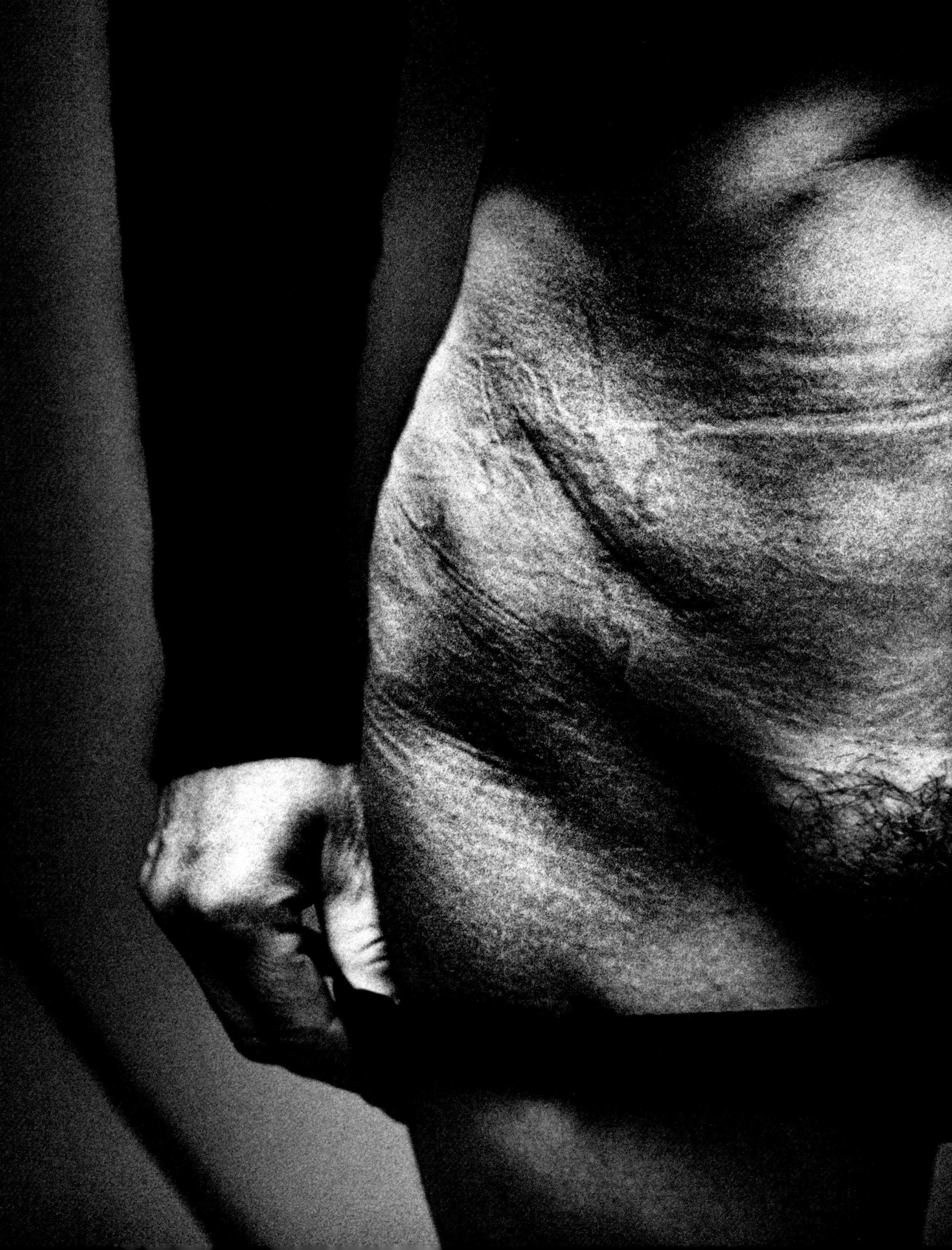

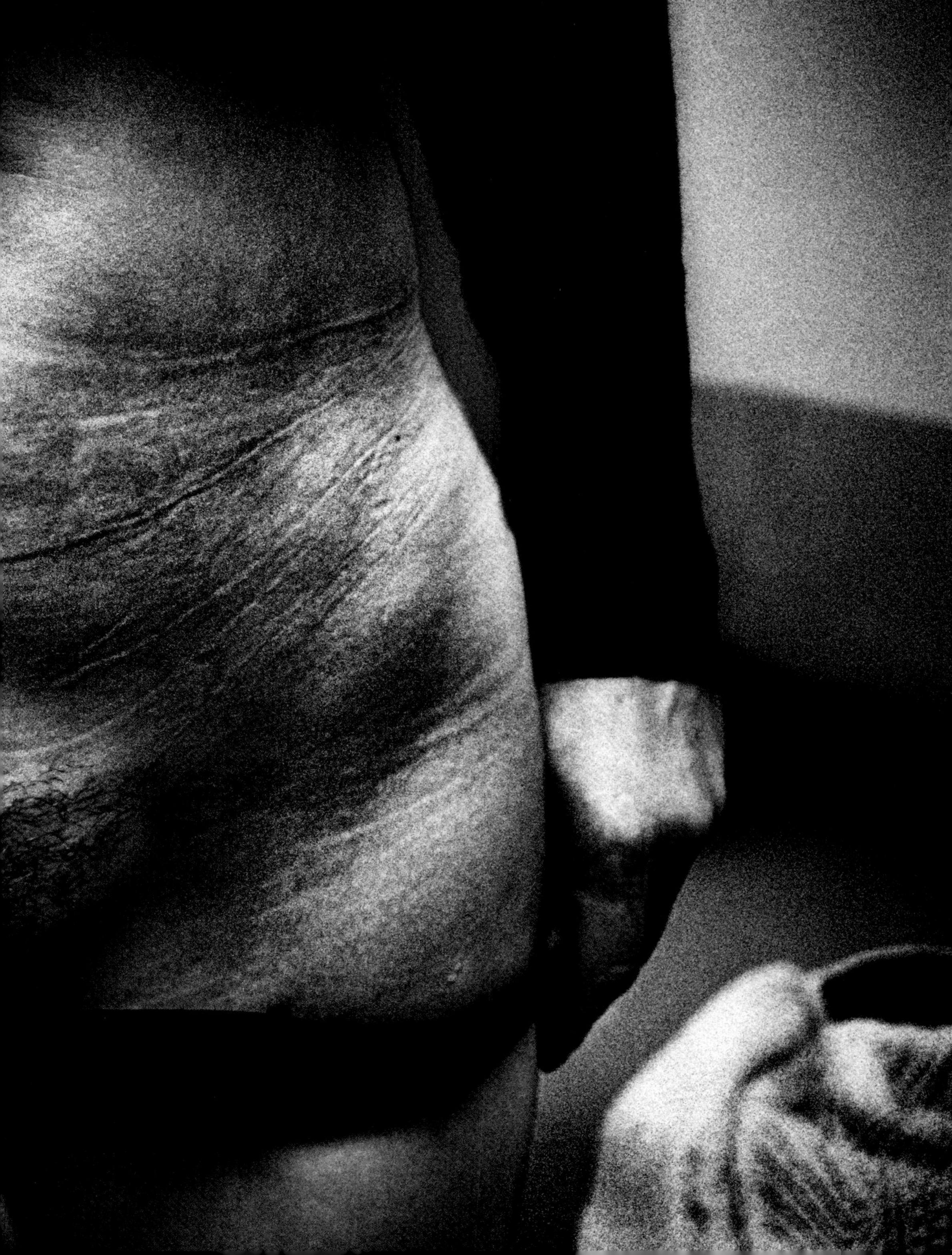

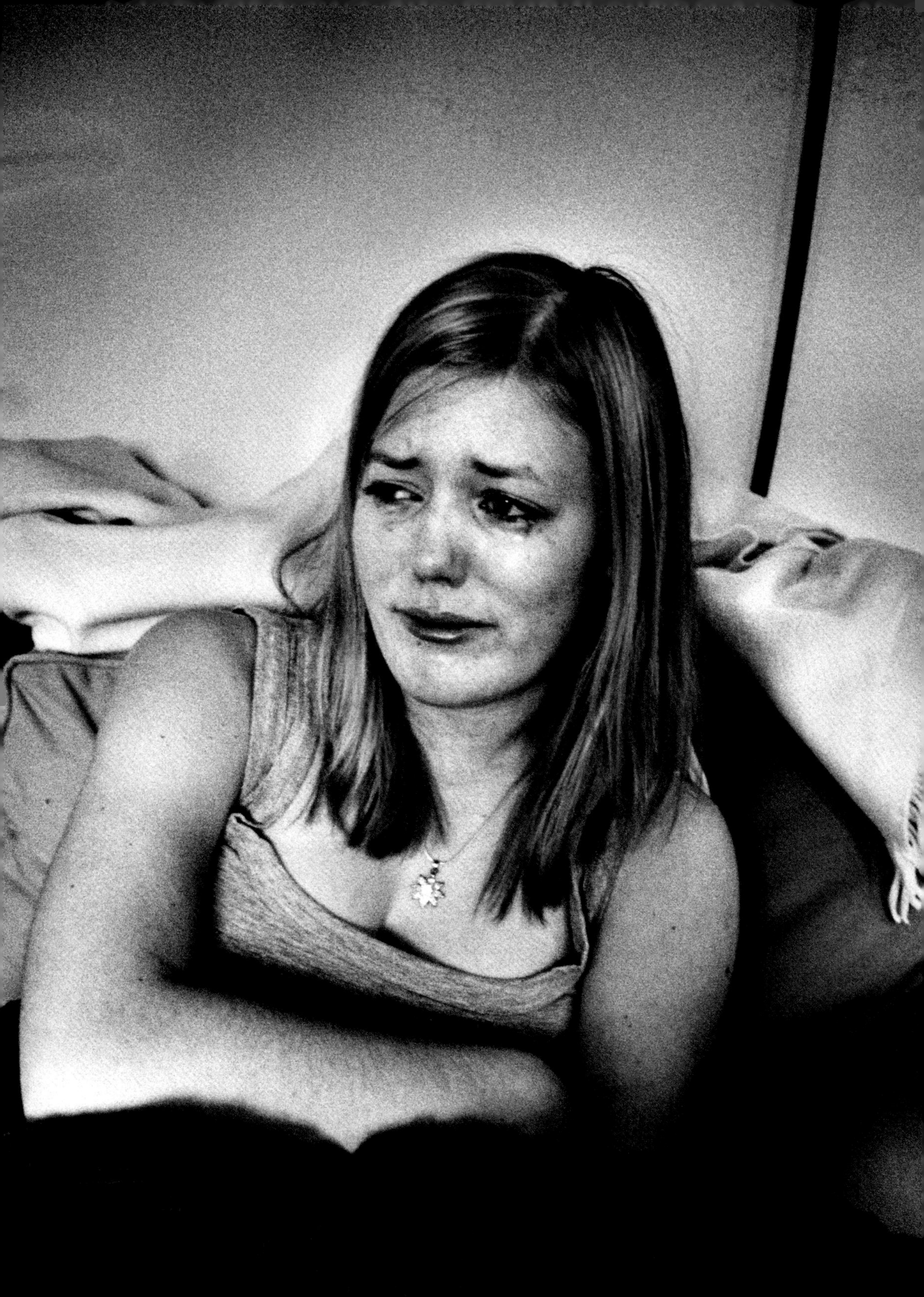

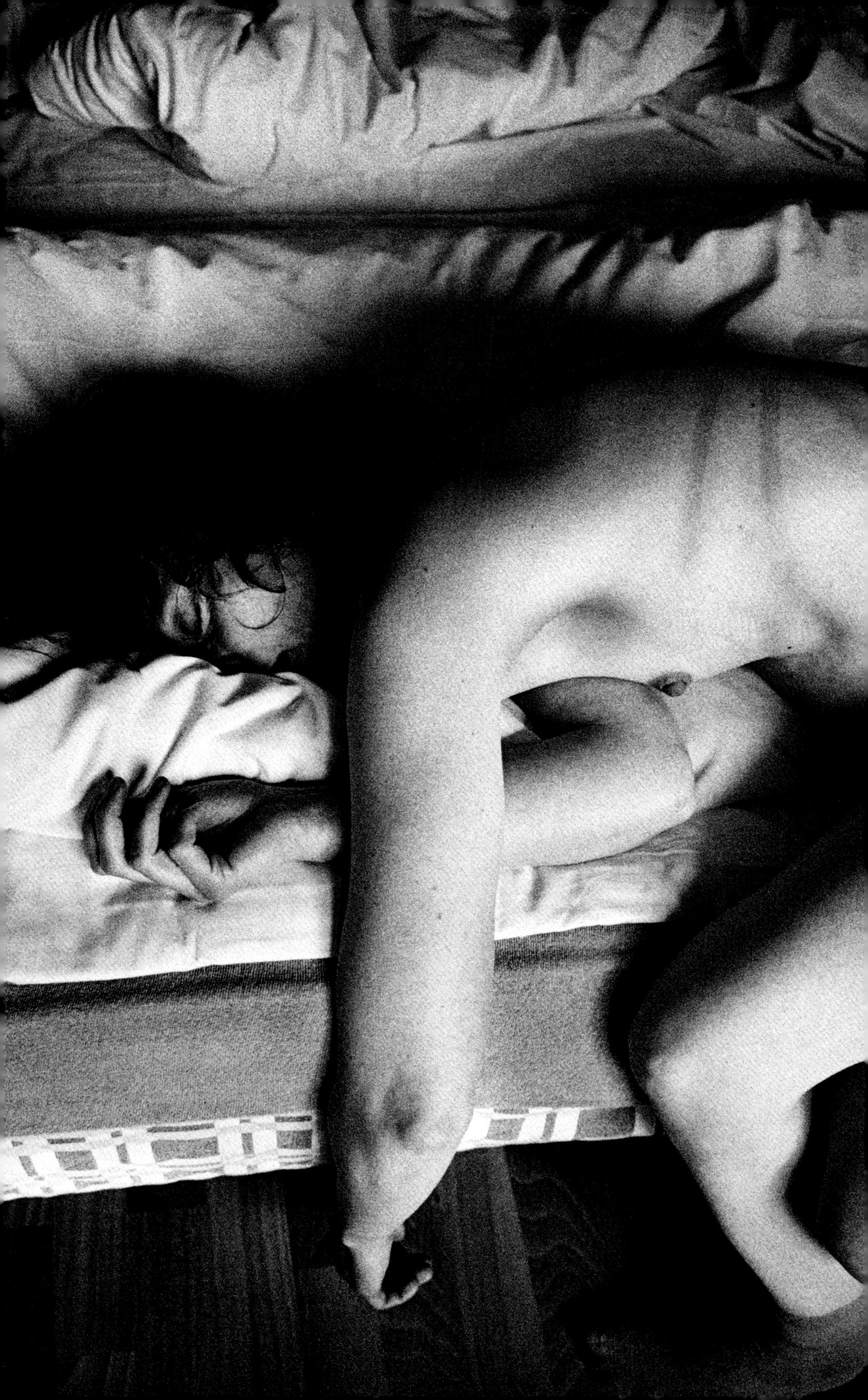

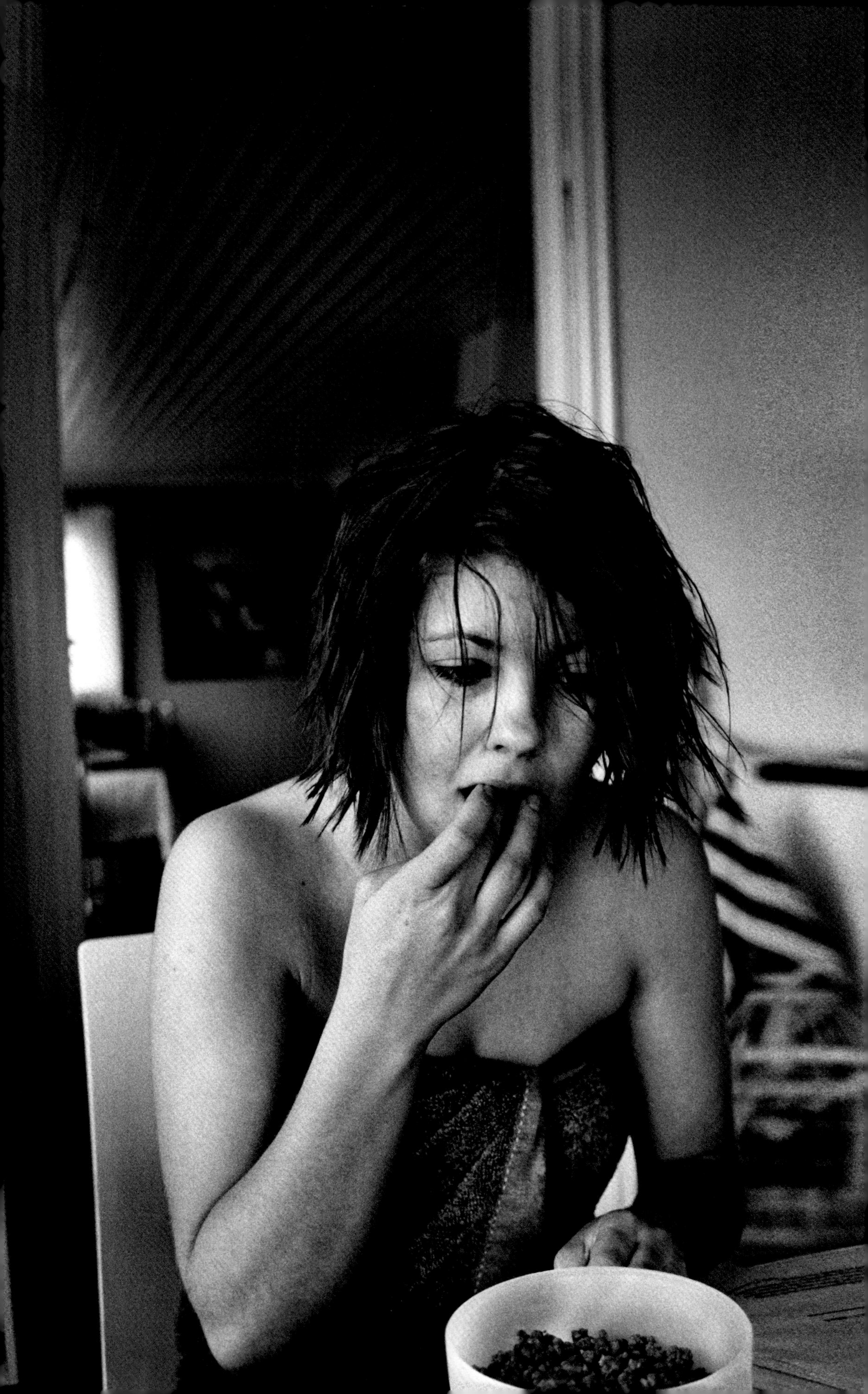

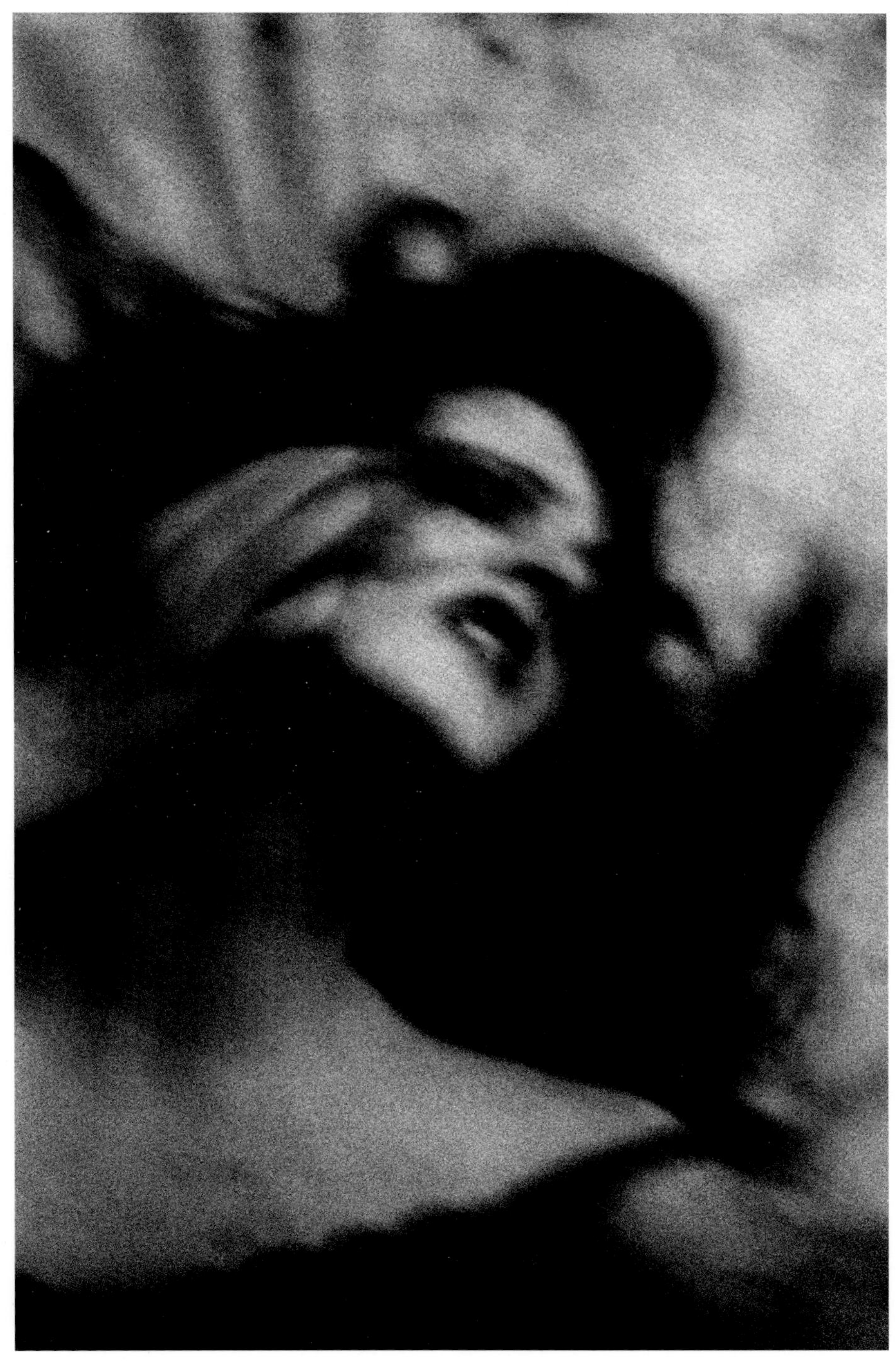

The loneliness we experience when surrounded by people is the loneliness we try our hardest to hide. On an unconscious level, I think I look for these sides to myself in the people around me. Those I'm close to, but also strangers I only have fleeting encounters with. These people become my mirrors; my way of showing those parts of me I'm trying to keep hidden.

My insecurities, dreams and longings. My happiness and sorrows, victories and downfalls. My loneliness.

Margaret M. de Lange

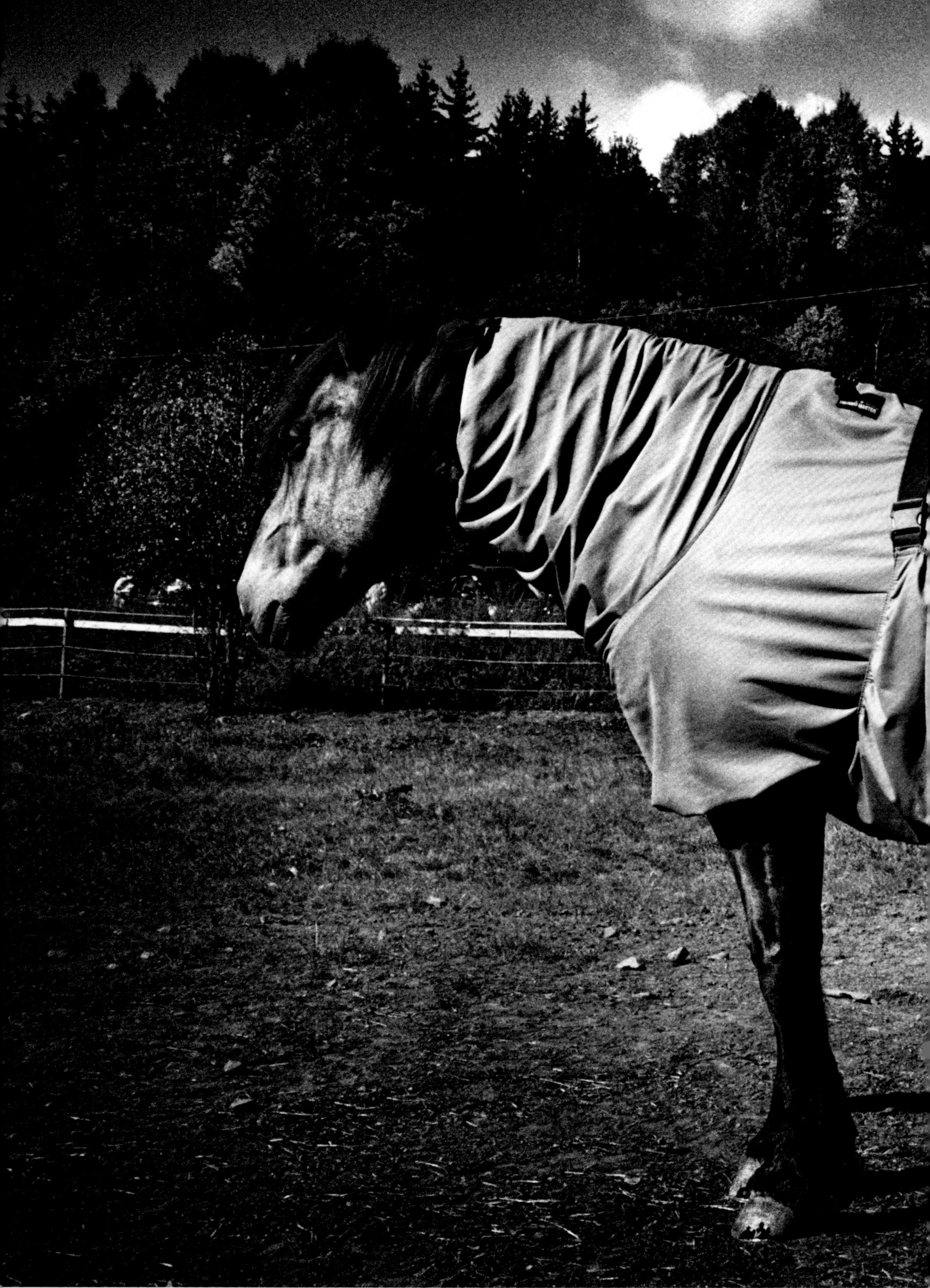

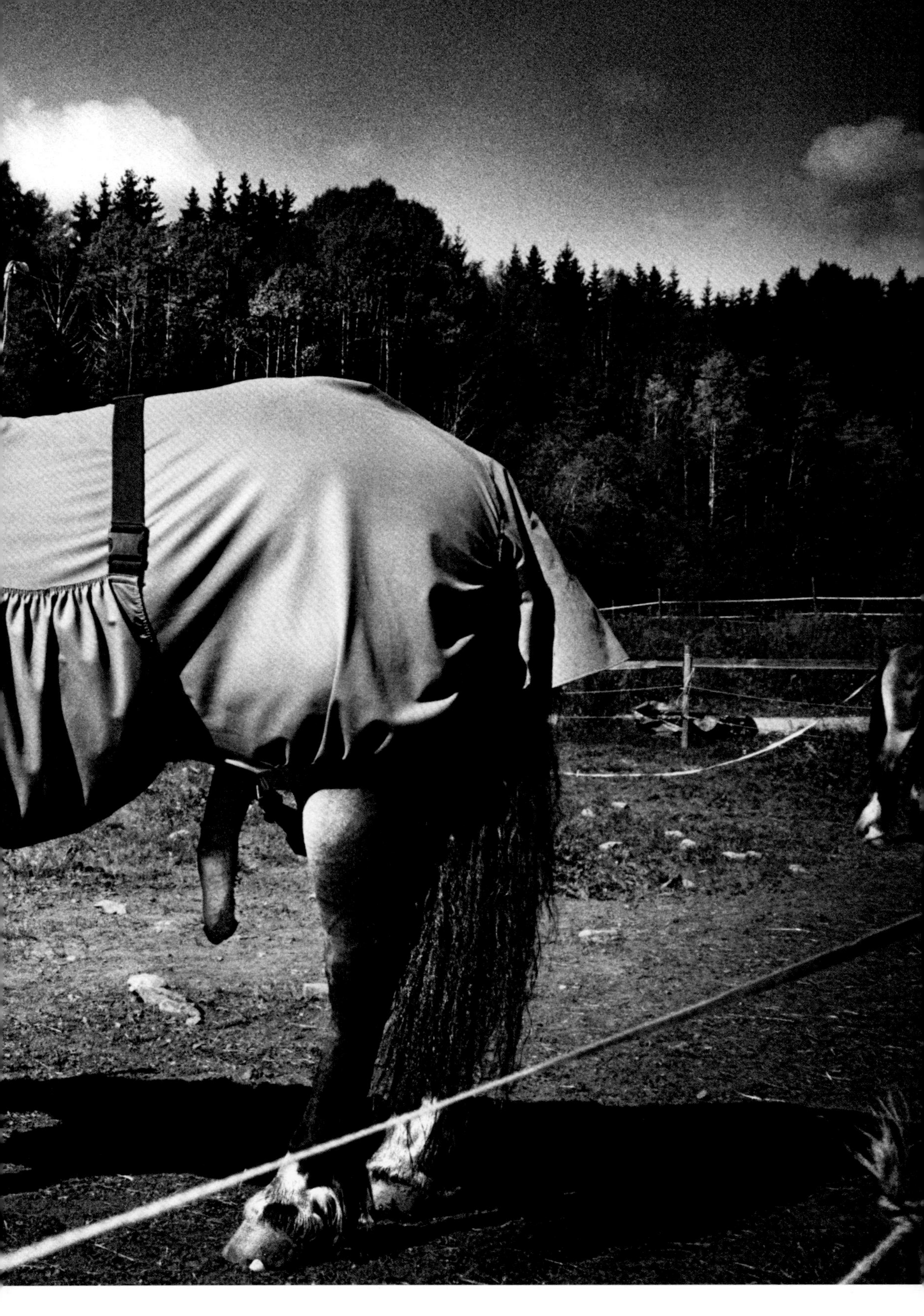

Thanks to:
My family
Anders Petersen
May B Langhelle
Gigi Giannuzzi
Arno Rafael Minkkinen
Isidor Aastrom
Stein Rune Kjuul

Published in Great Britain in 2011

Trolley Books
www.trolleybooks.com
Photographs © Margaret M. de Lange
Text © Arno Rafael Minkkinen
Design by Fruitmachinedesign.com

The right of Margaret M. de Lange to be identified as
the author of this work has been asserted by her in accordance with the
copyright, designs and patents act 1998.
A catalogue record for this book is available from the British Library.

ISBN 978-1-907112-35-5

All rights reserved. No part of this publication may be reproduced,
transmitted or stored in a retrieval system, in any form or by any means,
without permission in writing from Margaret M. de Lange and Trolley Ltd,
application for which must be made to Trolley Ltd.

Printed in Italy 2011 by Grafiche Antiga

'Surrounded by No One' is the second book by Margaret M. de Lange. Her first book
'Daughters' was published by Trolley in 2007, a photographic series of her daughters
which was also a runner up in the Leica Oskar Barnack award that year.